A HEARTBEAT
OF GRACE

To Kay...
God's richest blessings
to you! Embrace His
grace & embrace
YOUR story!
~KRISTIN STOECK
PS. 121

A HEARTBEAT OF GRACE

Experiencing More of God Through
The Trials and Triumphs in Life

KRISTIN STERK

First Printing: 2018

ISBN: 978-1986012713

Cover Design: Erik Peterson
Printed by CreateSpace

But he said to me, "My grace is sufficient for you, for my power is made perfect in weakness." Therefore I will boast all the more gladly about my weaknesses, so that Christ's power may rest on me.

~ 2 Corinthians 12:9

To my faithful Savior, Jesus Christ, who has given me the joy of salvation, and to whom I give all the glory for this book.

To my best friend and husband, Dan, who has helped me foster my dream of writing a book, and has added all the little details that has made this story what it is.

To my daughter and sidekick, Mazy Grace, who consistently makes me laugh, challenges me to grow in my faith and trust in God, and gives me all the hugs and kisses in the world.

To our two babies in Heaven; what a joyous reunion it will be.

To my dear friend, Brenda, who if it wasn't for her obedience and willingness to listen to the call of God in her life, I believe we would not have experienced the miracle of holding Mazy Grace in our arms.

CONTENTS

FOREWORD

Breath-taking.

When is the last time something so amazing, so delicate, so complex, yet so beautiful, simply made you stop what you are doing, take your breath away, and leave you in awe?

I suspect life's often-frantic pace leaves us little room to contemplate such potential wonders.

I invite you to create space in your life to take in the beauty and wonder-inducing awe of "A Heartbeat of Grace."

Kristin's heartbeat, a heart-and-soul story of resolve, set-backs, and victories, resembles a lot of our own heart's rhythm: the racing heart of adrenaline-driven passion, the steady heartbeat of daily trust, to the heart-stopping breathlessness of disappointment and loss... this is the heartbeat of grace.

The grace of this story is a fire-tested grace – one that plumbs the depths of loss and resurrects a weary soul. A grace that takes defect and disappointment and creates beauty. A grace that reveals God's all-surpassing power in the face of weakness again and again and again.

The Sterk family is very close to my heart. I've been privileged to know them as pastor and friend. And it's when you're invited in close to one's life story you get to feel deeply what they are going through; when victories come and setbacks knock them down. Walking close with the Sterks has led me to consider again, one of life's complexities, namely, the "why" for those who, with tender, well-meaning, love-filled hearts, seem to run into one roadblock after another, and often are left to wonder when the next "shoe will drop." This doesn't feel like grace. This doesn't feel like God. This doesn't seem fair.

But it is exactly in those seasons that the power of grace is revealed. For grace - true, life-changing grace - is revealed not in our own ability to "pull it together," or even to "keep it together," but shown through the steady hand of God taking each heart-stopping moment to shape something so amazing, so complex, yet so beautiful, out of what we would label "set-back or loss."

This weaving together of God's power and the life-surrendering trust of our own hearts is the story of "A Heartbeat of Grace."

Take a deep breath. Read. Wonder. Be in awe.

~ *Pastor Steven Zwart*
Unity CRC in Prinsburg, MN

CHAPTER 1

Way Back When

"Geur!"

(That was the nickname I was given by my high school basketball coach and teammates; it's an abbreviation of my maiden name, Geurink).

Coach called my name from down the bench. I ran down to the scorer's table, ready to jump into the game. As I stepped onto the court, I jogged to my position on the sideline, as the other team was in a defensive full court press. Suddenly, my hearing became muffled and my vision started to blur. I figured I was just dizzy because I went from sitting to running full tilt, at the snap of a finger. Not a big deal in my playbook.

Growing up in a farming community in West Michigan, life seemed simple. Any farmer would probably testify that this so-called simple life was anything but, with the stress of planting, harvest, milking, feedings, and those oh-so-early mornings — a simplicity that reflected a farmer's life, family, and faith.

My dad always found a job that needed to be done on the farm, from painting, to milking, to cleaning calf hutches. Just for a minute, imagine what could land on those walls? Well, that's what I scrubbed in preparation for a newborn calf. Throw in the opportunity to do this with my younger sister and it became a dream job, really. Saturday mornings we put on our designated barn clothes, shoved our feet into shoes held together with duct tape, grabbed our cassette radio player, and biked over to the farm a quarter mile down the road. After our jobs were complete, we'd come home smelling like the very place we came from, and though it permeated every part of our bodies, it strangely became one of the many comforting smells of home.

Nothing beat the smell of fresh cut hay, laundry swaying in the wind, and sunsets peeping through the gaps in between the silos that stood mightily in the distance. Long nights and early mornings journeyed together into this one simple life. It was a life I often took for granted.

As I grew older, so did my responsibilities on the farm, like milking cows. Milking wasn't one of the cleanest jobs, since often the cows did their bathroom duties while trying to get the milkers on. In fact, one time a cow kicked and a piece of manure went so far back into my mouth that the only option was to swallow it. My husband says that explains a lot about me today, but such was life. We didn't ask questions or complain (too much) because we all knew the jobs had to be done. It was the work ethic I was raised in. No questions asked.

I am quite proud of the culture and community I was brought up in. Our close family ties set the tone for the support and love I have received since the day I came into the world in 1983. My dad and mom deeply valued our family, which was evident in the way in which they nurtured, loved, and cared for my two sisters and me. I have an older and younger sister, and though we look like spitting images of each other, we are all different in our own ways, but couldn't get along better. That wasn't always the case growing up of course, but what siblings don't have their moments? To this day, I couldn't be more thankful for them and my family.

My parent's faith in God guided their every decision. Their reliance and upward eyes taught me to walk in the same way. A walk that trained me to see God working in the smallest of details.

On one particular evening, I remember standing in our garage, gazing at the clouds that were swiftly approaching. My dad stood next to me explaining what the different colors of the sky meant. He took the time to teach me the simple signs God was sending us through the different formations of the clouds. Green skies meant that a nasty storm was on the way (hail and maybe even tornadoes). Dark clouds with light skies meant a cold rainy day. A storm from the east? Brace yourself. Knowledge I would gain only from my dad being a farmer. I didn't realize it at the time, but learning to recognize and appreciate the power in these storms would be a life-long lesson.

Growing up, we were not permitted to watch TV on Sundays, purely to create an atmosphere of peace and quiet in our home. Though at about 2:00 on Sunday afternoons, I could hear my dad turn the TV on to check the score of a game. Well, that "checking" turned into an hour, which then turned into a time of watching sports (mainly basketball) together.

Though by the time I was in middle school, it didn't take long for me to want to recreate what those basketball players were doing on TV. After watching a game, I would lace up my shoes and run down to our own little basketball court that was an old cement slab where my parent's old mobile home sat. The more I watched and the more I played, the more basketball became my life.

On a family vacation, I found a t-shirt that I had to have. The bold letters printed across the front "Basketball Is Life," put words to the dreams I had in my head. That shirt became THE shirt I wore in middle school. Let me tell you, I was trendy, with my wind suit pants, pony-tailed hair, curled bangs, and black Nike high tops to complete the fashion trend.

Every Saturday afternoon, I sat glued to the television watching *NBA Inside Stuff* with Ahmad Rashad. Thank goodness for the TV guide that was sent in the newspaper because I then could plan my day accordingly. While watching basketball games, I would single out one player, memorize their every move, then run down to the cement slab to perfect their every move. Meanwhile, during our routine Sunday afternoon naptime, I pored over *Sports Illustrated* magazines, dreaming of becoming a star basketball player.

Basketball became my life. Given my height, this love for basketball was almost expected. In 8th grade, I topped the charts at 5 feet 11 ¾ inches. Needless to say, I wasn't short by any measure of the stick. I was tall, skin and bones, and just plain awkward, but I didn't care. In my spiral notebook journal, I recorded all of my dreams and desires as a basketball player. I distinctly remember writing, "I want to be the first woman in the NBA." If you're going to dream, dream big, right? I was determined to play next to the likes of Kobe Bryant and Kevin Garnett. After all, Kevin had the same initials as I did: "KG." I was destined.

The more time I spent nurturing my dream of being the first woman in the NBA, the more obsessed I became with the sport. I placed high expectations on myself for greatness, which then others did too, since I was given that gift of height.

During one particular game against our rival school my sophomore year of high school, I had one of those shining moments that I dreamed would end up on one of ESPN's top 10 plays. I stole the ball from the other team and nervously ran down the court, dribbling the ball, in hopes of getting that fast break layup. A girl from the other team stepped into my lane, and as I tripped over her foot, my right rib cage slammed into her left knee. As I lied there gasping and groaning for a breath, my vision blurred and I became desperate for oxygen. Once I caught my breath, I knew I was done for the game, as I was helped off the court to the bench.

A day later, x-rays showed a fractured rib, which meant a few weeks of no playing. It was a devastating blow, in more ways than one. Unfortunately, there was no easy fix for a fractured rib, except rest, time, and a whole lot of Ibuprofen. And once I did come back, the season was never the same. Every rebound and jump was hindered with pain.

It was an unexpected injury, but in the end was an injury that only bought me more time.

CHAPTER 2

Beginning of the End

During basketball tryouts my junior year of high school, my coach jogged with me in the back of the pack, as we ran a timed mile. He kindly asked if I had done any conditioning during the summer, recognizing that I was gasping for air. Honestly, I was running five miles a day, at a pace that I thought was decent; maybe not on par with Olympic track stars, but pretty good for a 16-year-old high school basketball player. As I saw my teammates sprinting past me, my mind wondered, "What did I do wrong?" In thinking about my coach's question, I could feel my throat getting tight as I choked back tears. I had a high level of respect for him and didn't want to do anything to disappoint him. Mentally I became frustrated as my body was telling me, "Either you choose to stop, or I will stop for you." I reassured my coach I did condition at home, and to my surprise, it was enough. I made the team.

Truth be told, that summer before tryouts, I felt this unrecognizable tug to not play. I wasn't sure what it was and I wasn't sure it was from God, so I ignored it. What high schooler would quit the game they loved? Why would God ask me to quit the game I loved? So like I said, I ignored it.

I didn't get a lot of playing time that season, due to the fact that there were two senior centers who were better than I was. Though what I loved most was just being part of the team. From practice, to the bus rides and games, I loved every moment. Basketball was still my life, despite not playing much, and I was just learning the joys of being part of a team.

Sadly enough, I didn't realize what basketball was doing to my life. Obsession would be putting it lightly as the sport consumed everything I thought about and did. A life lived for a sport that could be taken away from me at any moment.

Early in the summer before my junior year of high school, I had my routine sports physical. As my family practitioner, Dr. Van Dyke, intently listened to my heart, she heard a faint heart murmur. Murmurs are the abnormal sounds your blood makes while working through the heart. A normal heartbeat would consist of a "lubb-dupp" type sound. With a murmur, a doctor can hear a distinct swishing or whooshing sound that coincides with that normal heartbeat, making it an abnormal sound. I had never heard of a murmur, but I figured if the murmur was pretty silent like my doctor said, how serious could it be?

Dr. Van Dyke referred me to the local hospital to have an echocardiogram (ECHO), which is basically an ultrasound of the heart, and then have a cardiologist read the results, just to be sure. Curiously, Dr. Van Dyke never received the report of what the ECHO showed. After she realized in September that no report was

9

received, she was a bit furious, but nevertheless, obtained the report from the local cardiologist that stated I was just fine.

Dr. Van Dyke isn't only a doctor, but a respectable woman of God. It is evident in her practice that she works not for her own glory, but for God's alone, treating her patients as if we were her own. Even though she encouraged me to play that season, she wasn't comfortable with "just fine." She suggested I schedule an appointment with another cardiology specialist, so that I could be seen in person and not just have my ECHO looked at. My appointment was scheduled for December 1, 2000; that was the earliest I could get in.

I had been playing basketball since I was a little girl. How would a health issue all of a sudden pop up now? Especially with my heart? I had done countless sprints up and down that court. At times I tired quickly, but I assumed that since I was taller and therefore weighed more, that it would take more out of me.

Now, let me take you back to that scene I introduced at the beginning:

"Geur!"

Coach called my name from down the bench. I ran down to the scorer's table, ready to jump into the game. As I stepped onto the court, I jogged to my position on the sideline, as the other team was in a defensive full court press. Suddenly, my hearing became muffled and my vision started to blur. I figured I was just dizzy because I went from sitting to running full tilt, at the snap of a finger. Not a big deal in my playbook.

The week of my appointment proved to be one for the books. On Monday, it was my 17th birthday. On Tuesday, the elections for Winterfest hostess occurred, and I learned my name was on the ballot. On Wednesday, I found out I was chosen to represent the junior class at Winterfest. On Thursday, I tried out for the shotput team and actually was decent at it, even though I had never thrown before. Friday was my heart appointment, with our end of the season basketball party at night.

Here are some further details about what this all meant. Being named Winterfest hostess for the junior class, which was our high school's form of homecoming since we didn't have football, was shocking. Let me paint this picture for you. I was no one special. I wasn't a star basketball player. I didn't hang out with the popular crowd. By no means did I wear Tommy Hilfiger clothing. I surely didn't define "cool" by any sense of the word.

I was one of those girls who didn't have just one select group of friends that I hung out with exclusively. I had a core group of friends, but enjoyed sitting with other people in the hallways during lunch too. On weekends, I didn't hang out with one particular person. I didn't care about status or what group you were in. How somebody looked on the outside didn't matter to me as much as the inside did.

So to think that anyone would vote for me to represent the junior class came as a complete surprise; granted I was done wearing my wind suit pants and t-shirt combo every day to school, but I just never imagined myself being chosen for something like this. Little did I know that this simple event would encourage me to keep going, despite the news I was soon to receive.

On that Friday afternoon, December 1, 2000, I had my scheduled appointment with the heart specialists, to confirm that my heart murmur was nothing more than a murmur. I was mainly excited to get out of school early since that rarely happened. I was never late for school and can't even remember going home early because I was sick. So getting out of school early was something out of the ordinary.

So at the age of 17 and now 6′1″, I walked into the pediatric office. Parenting magazines and children's books lined the shelves, and it was obvious I was a little old to be there. Toys covered the floor and the wall décor screamed "children's office." When my name was called, I walked into the room with my red Champion basketball shorts, tennis shoes, and t-shirt. The nurse encouraged me to wear gym-type clothing, which as a basketball player wasn't a problem since that was my go-to attire. While I laid on the patient table, a baby mobile hung above as my feet draped over the edge; the nurse and I could only laugh at how out of place this all seemed. Even though I was still a "kid," it was obvious that this office wasn't accustomed to seeing 6′1″ kids.

I laid there on the table as a medical imaging technician started to prepare me for an ECHO, where the doctors would be able to get a better picture of what my heart looked like. As the technician gently moved the probe over my heart, she became noticeably quiet. She seemed to have abruptly left the room, so I glanced over at my mom and saw a look of sheer worry in her eyes. The technician came back into the room with a doctor and started whispering back and forth. I was getting the feeling that this was no longer considered a "normal" checkup.

After the technician finished the test, the doctor asked if we could meet him in a conference room. Why a conference room to discuss the results? Was this routine? Were all of the patient rooms so full that we had to meet in a different room?

My mom and I cautiously walked into the room. I was asked to take a seat at the head of the table as other doctors and technicians gathered around. The doctor began to explain that they found an abnormal condition called an anomalous left coronary artery off the pulmonary artery (ALCAPA).

ALCAPA is a very rare heart condition. About 1% of babies are born with a congenital heart defect in general, which equals about 1 in 40,000 in the United States.[1] Specifically, out of that 1%, only about 0.25-0.5% of them have ALCAPA,[2] which is an extremely low percentage. If the defect is left untreated, it has an infant mortality rate at about 90% that increases the older the person gets.[3] How I was still alive at 17, was only by God's grace. As rare as it is to find ALCAPA in a newborn baby, it is even more rare to discover it in a teenager; especially one that was still living a "normal" life.

So what does having ALCAPA mean? When my heart was developing, my left coronary artery, which normally brings oxygen-rich blood from the aorta to the left side of the heart muscle, was instead connected to the pulmonary artery, causing deoxygenated blood to flow to the left side of my heart. The only way to fix this abnormality was through an open heart surgery. If left untouched, the tissue in my heart would continue to die from lack of oxygen and eventually result in a heart attack. I was a walking time bomb and my heart could give out at any time.

After hearing this, I thought okay, so we just fix it! That part didn't concern me. Then reality hit. He proceeded to tell me that I had to quit doing anything that required physical exertion. That meant no basketball, or any other sport for that matter. Ironically, remember that the day before I had signed up for the shotput team? Being part of a team was what I loved so much about basketball, and now I had to basically be a couch potato.

The doctors wanted to verify that there were no surprises during surgery or any other issues with my heart, so the next step would be to have a heart catheterization in two weeks to get a better image of my heart.

As my mom and I stepped into the elevator and walked back to our car, I could see it took everything in her to not completely break down in tears. At the time, I didn't understand the severity of the situation and to be honest, I just thought it was a little glitch.

The drive home was rather silent, except for the sound of sniffles, as my mom's tears streamed down her cheeks. Seeing her tears caused my tears to start falling. It finally occurred to me that I wasn't going to be playing basketball anymore.

My mom dropped me off at school so I could grab my car and head straight to the basketball party at the bowling alley. She asked if I'd be okay and if I still wanted to go, but of course I did! Little did I know though, that it would be the last time I would be at an event labeled as a basketball player.

Soon after arriving at the bowling alley, a teammate asked how my appointment went; I immediately broke down. I definitely put her in an awkward situation because that wasn't what she expected to see and I surely didn't expect to lose it. More teammates gathered around as I told them that I was done playing basketball. The coaches then overheard us talking and were just as shocked at the news. How could this be real?

For me, the rest of the evening was over-shadowed with this reality that my life would never be the same.

I went to bed that night confused and frustrated. My pillow became wet with tears, as I slowly processed the news and replayed the events of the day in my mind. Why would God choose a heart condition, at the age of 17, to shake up my life? As I reflected on what the cardiologist had said, that the damage my heart showed, could possibly be lifelong, I surprisingly felt this indescribable peace in my spiritual heart that I'd never felt before. Maybe this was more than just about quitting basketball.

Two weeks later, I had my scheduled heart catheterization. The results showed that there were no further issues and that open heart surgery would be scheduled for January 17, 2001.

What 17-year-old plans to have open heart surgery? I thought only the really sick had to have that type of surgery. I was supposed to be conditioning for track, lifting weights for next year's upcoming basketball season, and hanging out with my friends. My only worries should be about where I was going to sit at lunch and what guy I liked at that given time.

My parents did an incredible job of protecting me from the realities of what open heart surgery really entailed, like the severity, the pain, and the after-effects. Though I didn't know this until years later, the month between finding out about my heart condition and the actual surgery, my mom struggled. For a week she cried daily, yet I don't have one memory of it. Even sitting around the dinner table as a family became difficult for her. I can only imagine the pain my parents felt as they envisioned their teenage daughter going in for open heart surgery, not knowing what the outcome would be.

Since Christmas was approaching, the cardiologist mentioned to my parents that some families make the Christmas before a surgery like mine even more special, knowing it could be my last. Again, I had no clue that my parents were given that advice. What difficult words to hear, during such a joyous season.

Despite the sadness and frustration I felt, God had already rolled up His sleeves. The time in between finding out I needed surgery and the actual day of it, I found in myself a faith I didn't know I had. There was this God-peace that filled me, which I didn't know existed, until it was called up to bat. Everything in my life up until that point seemed easy and my faith was never put to the test.

In 5th grade, I remember writing my teacher a letter (my love for writing started way back then), telling her that I'd accepted Jesus into my heart. I had grown up in a Christian home, and everything in life revolved around faith. As far back as I can remember, I had always believed that Jesus died for me, which was a prayer I know I said as a little girl, but at that moment, facing a major surgery at 17, my faith finally became real to me.

The night before the surgery, my pastor came over to encourage, give reassurance, and pray for my parents and me. It was a bit somber because it was all becoming so real. As my pastor read Psalm 121, a new understanding of that passage came to fruition. For me, the words of that Psalm meant something deeper, even though I had heard it plenty of times before:

Psalm 121
1 I lift up my eyes to the mountains –
  where does my help come from?
2 My help comes from the Lord,
  the Maker of heaven and earth.
3 He will not let your foot slip –
  he who watches over you will not slumber;
4 indeed, he who watches over Israel
  will neither slumber nor sleep.
5 The Lord watches over you –
  the Lord is your shade at your right hand;

6 the sun will not harm you by day,
   nor the moon by night.
7 The Lord will keep you from all harm –
   he will watch over your life;
8 the Lord will watch over your coming and going
   both now and forevermore.

I read that Psalm one more time before I went to bed that night, knowing from that point on, it wouldn't only be a statement for my life that night and the following weeks, but also for years to come.

CHAPTER 3

Open Heart Surgery #1

It was a brisk winter morning on Wednesday, January 17, 2001. The dark and cold feeling of the hospital with the lights still dim at 6:00 a.m., made the situation feel all the more grim. As we sat in the waiting room, nurses came by offering their hugs and well-wishes, realizing that this wasn't how life was supposed to be.

I sat in the chair with my gym bag of clothes sitting next to me, reflecting on my 17 years of life. Up until that point, I thought I was invincible. My life was never put into question, until now. Would that day be my last? Was this a life I was proud of? If I had a do-over, what would I change?

My thoughts quickly jumped back to reality as a nurse stepped forward and gently called out, "Kristin, we're ready for you!"

And it all began. At any moment, my parents would've traded places with me in a heartbeat. Literally. Though they too felt that overwhelming peace, which clearly was only from God.

Before I had time to process it all, I was getting wheeled to the operating room.

"Kristin, how are you feeling? Are you ready? We're going to put IV's in you. How old are you? You're so young." Questions and comments filled the operating room, as the doctors and nurses tried to take my mind off the inevitable. I decided to joke around with them, which made it feel more like a New Year's Eve party, except the party goers wore surgical attire instead of ballroom gowns.

Then, through his surgical mask, the anesthesiologist started the countdown: "10, 9, 8..." My last thought I could remember thinking was, "Will I see my Heavenly Father?"

My surgeon was an old man who planned to retire soon, but with steady hands, he sawed through my sternum and opened up my chest cavity to gain access to my heart. Once inside, with a scalpel, he meticulously detached my coronary artery from the pulmonary artery and then was able to reattach it to my aorta where it should've been in the first place. In order to perform this six hour long surgery, the doctors had to stop my heart, deflate my lungs, and connect me to a heart-lung machine that would circulate oxygen-rich blood through my body, keeping me alive, while my heart wasn't pumping.

The surgery was successful and the surgeon was able to do exactly what he had set out to do. The first couple of hours after the surgery were the most critical, since my heart could start leaking or just stop beating at any time.

Coming out of surgery, I vividly remember trying to breathe on my own. Imagine trying to get a full breath through a tiny straw, while your throat and lungs are filled with mucus. I gagged on the ventilator that up until that point was breathing for me. Through groans, I begged my mom to take it out. I grasped at it, but my lungs weren't ready to function on their own yet, so the nurses had to tie down my arms to prevent me from pulling it out.

I will always remember my mom's touch. Her gentle hands, holding mine, telling me I was going to be okay. When I first opened my eyes, there were countless people in the room, but I distinctly remember seeing my parents. Familiar faces that gave me a determination to make it through those first few hours.

Day two presented to be a struggle between the pain in my abdomen where my three chest tubes were inserted to drain excess fluid around my heart, the burn of the potassium that was too quickly injected through an IV, coughing that felt like a dumbbell was dropped on my sternum, and difficulty sleeping. It was a tough day to say the least. I started to wonder, can I really do this?

By day three, I turned a corner; endurance and optimism filled my bones. Even though I was still unable to lift my own head, my mobility increased. Having those three long rubber chest tubes that were sticking out of my abdomen removed, was a kind reminder that I was one step closer to going home.

While walking around the pediatric ICU floor that third day, realities of being in the ICU set in. While doing my required laps, I witnessed young children's lives being held together by tubes and machines. It was a difficult situation to witness when their parents looked at me with despair-filled eyes. I knew I'd be going home the next day or two, but for those children, the future seemed grim.

As I made my laps and gingerly walked by the nurse's station, one by one they came from around their desks and asked how I was doing so well (apparently they thought I was doing better than expected). I stuttered and was without words - probably for the first time in my life.

The only explanation I had was God. It was then, while standing and leaning up against that nurse's station, that I realized God could maybe use this story, to touch others' lives. Maybe this story, this surgery, had a greater purpose than what I imagined? After that short, yet life-altering conversation with them about my progress, faith, and God's grace, I headed back to my ICU room. That room had become my home and was beginning to teach me that my life would be defined less by what those four walls limited me to, but more by the power of what God was doing in and through my life.

The next day, day four, I was able to go home. My neck IV still had to be removed, but that was the last tube that connected me to my hospital room. The doctor had gone over all of the rules and restrictions for life at home, and thankfully my parents were there to digest it all because to be quite frank, I wasn't very attentive! I was just excited to be going home!

As I was wheeled out of the ICU room that was my home for the past four days, with gifts, stuffed animals, and balloons in hand, I felt I was officially on the road to recovery.

Recovery at home was frustrating at times, yet each day brought progress. Sleeping in a regular bed posed a challenge because I couldn't lie flat, due to the pressure it put on my rib cage. My mom became a pro at propping up pillows, as she "recreated" a hospital bed so I could sleep upright. Every morning I had to call for her to get me up since I still was unable to lift my head up on my own. It was a rather humbling situation to say the least.

The tender love and care my parents provided for me during that whole ordeal was a parental example that I've been able to take with me to this day. They offered this gentle balance of ensuring I was comfortable, emotionally stable, and making sure I didn't overdo it, which in the end, sped up my recovery. It was all a new normal for me that I was still trying to navigate. Yet they continued to protect me from the true realities of what this surgery really meant: possible life-long heart issues. At that time, nobody knew the effects my congenital heart condition would have on my life. Knowing that they just wanted the best for me and to just love my teenage years, is something I am still grateful to them for, to this day.

By that next Monday (1 ½ weeks after surgery), I was getting restless and felt ready to go back to school. My mom called the doctor and they said that if I felt up to it, I could go back.

Was I up to it? You bet I was! The love and care my school gave was incredible. My classmates acted as my body guards; often I had two guys standing next to me, protecting me from getting bumped in the hallways, since my sternum was still broken. I went to school full-time the rest of that week and never looked back.

I had a few more doctors' appointments throughout the next few weeks and then slowly weaned off those as well. Probably the most frustrating part during those next few months was not being able to drive, which as a teenager was like telling me I couldn't have a life. At 17 years old, I just wanted to have the freedom to drive and hang out with my friends. I had already felt I lost a bit of my life by having to give up sports. I didn't want to have to give up driving too. Thankfully though, that time passed quickly.

Three weeks after surgery was Winterfest night. When I was named hostess for the junior class, that meant I was to get all dressed up (like a prom), and be a part of a skit that our class had put together. Leading up to that night, I was a little nervous because I still had a long ways to go recovery-wise. The bone in my sternum hadn't completely fused back together, yet despite the metal wires woven throughout to hold it together. The scar running down the center of my chest looked alarming as it was still raised and dark purple in color. When I looked in the mirror, it was the first thing I saw. What would others think? Even though the scars told an amazing story, it was something that as a young teenage girl, I was insecure about.

My mom felt the pain I had of feeling self-conscious about my scars. I had dreamed of wearing a white dress to Winterfest, but I wasn't able to go dress shopping, since my range of motion and endurance hadn't fully returned. I couldn't even put my own socks on, let alone zip up the back of a dress in a dressing room. So my mom graciously took the time to sew me the most beautiful gown, my dream gown, for me to wear that special night. She even made a little scarf for me to wear around my neck so my scar would be hidden. That beautiful gown meant so much to me, but the hands that sewed it meant even more. As a gift, my aunts hired two people to come to our house to do my hair and makeup that night, since we all knew I wouldn't be able to do it myself. I could barely lift my arms above my head, let alone do my own hair. What a gift that was.

That day, Winterfest day, I felt beautiful again. I felt like a million dollars. Scars and all.

My parents and I weren't sure I would be able to walk with my host out to center court during half time of the boys' basketball game, and we assumed I'd be pushed in a wheelchair instead. That night though, I became determined to not be bound by two wheels.

I walked the whole way to center court, hanging onto my host, without missing a step. It was the most surreal experience when three weeks prior, I was lying lifeless on a surgery table. The crowd stood, clapping and cheering. It didn't have anything to do with me, but had everything to do with what God had done. He had taken a physically broken heart, but in the end, healed a physical *and* spiritual one in the process. The work that God had done; now that deserved a standing ovation.

CHAPTER 4

A Change in Love

After my surgery, I felt my life began a new chapter - a starting over, if you would. As I was trying to navigate what my life would look like with no basketball and no sports, God changed my heart from a love for basketball to a love for Him. Basketball was all I knew, and I had let it define who I was. Now it was time to let GOD define me and redefine my passions.

During my senior year, my English teacher, Mrs. Hoekema, pulled me aside and asked if I would be interested in helping with the service projects my high school was involved in. I always enjoyed missions and reaching out to those who just needed a little extra love and support, but I hadn't been a part of many outreach opportunities up to that point.

It didn't take much convincing for me to accept the invitation and soon I was more than involved.

I ended up being maybe a bit overcommitted, but looking back, it was all worth it. I helped run an afterschool program and Saturday events at an inner-city church and ministry in Grand Rapids, Michigan, called Clancy Street Ministries. I also helped lead a Wednesday night chapel service at a homeless shelter once a month and assisted in planning chapels at my school. To say the least, I found my new niche. A new passion and a new Kristin.

Since I wasn't able to play basketball my senior year, I was the team manager instead, and was still able to travel with the team, which helped fulfill my love for the game. I could just be crazy ole Kristin. I didn't have to worry about the games, but desired to keep the spirits of my teammates high. Before each game, I would write each of the girls an encouragement note with a Bible verse, a quote, or just words of affirmation. If I couldn't cheer on my teammates as a player, this was the next best thing.

As for the track team, instead of doing the shotput, I was able to take measurements. Looking back, when God nudged my family doctor, Dr. Van Dyke, with that "still, small voice," it was all in His perfect timing. If she hadn't pressed the issue and followed up with the heart specialists, more than likely I would've become a part of the statistics of young athletes that unexplainably collapse dead on the court or field, only to learn post-mortem that there was a fatal heart condition.

Remember when I fractured a rib during my sophomore year? I ended up sitting out for a few weeks, which was part of God's perfect plan. Remember too, that my junior year, I didn't play much because there were two tall seniors ahead of me? Seniors always played first and with two playing the same position I did, playing time was at a minimum. Again, all part of God's perfect plan.

I have to say that I am incredibly grateful to my parents for their sacrifice to send me to the high school they did – Unity

Christian High School in Hudsonville, Michigan. I know it's cliché to say that if it wasn't for the teachers, administrators, and my fellow classmates, I wouldn't be the person I am today, but it really is true. God used the various opportunities my high school offered and mostly the people who invested in me daily, to form me into the person He desired.

It was also my parents who nurtured that love for others in me. They were examples of a selfless love to me. They encouraged me to fuel my passions and to serve people and God. I drove from the comforts of the country to the roughest parts of the city to do the things I loved. My parents never said no, even when I'm sure they were nervous allowing their 17-year-old daughter to go to a part of the city where most people wouldn't choose to go to. Because of their faith in God and their encouragement to do what my "new" heart was made to do, I feel I am thriving today, being who God created me to be.

Not only was my physical heart healed, but my spiritual heart as well. Open heart surgery tested my faith, but having to discover a new life and a new passion brought my faith to a whole new level. The only way for God to heal both of my hearts was to open our eyes to a congenital heart disease that I carried with me for 17 years.

The inner city ministry where I volunteered not only became a part of my life, but also a part of my heart. The children there touched me and brought tears to my spiritual heart, each time I had to drive away from the projects where they lived. I went to bed at night thinking about them. I woke up wondering how I could love them more. That passion only deepened the more I became involved.

And that passion soon became my calling.

After high school, I attended Reformed Bible College, now known as Kuyper College in Grand Rapids, Michigan. I started my freshman year as a youth ministry major, but after just a few short months, I switched to social work. A social work professor sat by me at the lunch table one day, trying to convert me. You'd think that at a small Christian college, when we talk about conversions, we'd be talking about a similar conversion as the Apostle Paul. However, the conversion here was in changing majors. There seemed to be a friendly rivalry between the different professors over which major was the "best," and there was an unspoken competition to get students to switch over to the "best" major.

The more I considered and listened to his convincing, the more I realized he was right. The type of work I wanted to do in the inner city, and the issues I would be dealing with, were social work related. So why not have the best of both worlds – ministering to youth while having the knowledge of how to deal with the social issues through having a degree in social work? So I converted.

That decision to change my major set me up for some incredible opportunities and experiences. I was still involved with Clancy Street Ministries and ended up working for them as an intern for three summers. I had to raise my own funds, but it was worth every penny. As the saying often goes in ministry, "I wasn't in it for the money," and I truly wasn't. I probably spent all I raised on the gas driving back and forth. Maybe I should've cared more about making money to save for college, but my dad always needed help with milking cows and cleaning calf hutches. Really, it was the best of both worlds. I was able to work with the people and kids I loved at the ministry center, but also work with my family on the farm.

Those kids at the ministry truly became my kids. I would hop in the 15 passenger van and start driving down the streets, looking for kids to come to the day programs I had organized. Kids came running full tilt to the van because they knew that meant a program was going on and there was something to do. There were definitely some challenges while working there, like dealing with kids who came from abusive homes, parents with addictions, and kids with behavioral issues to name a few, but those kids knew the ministry center was a safe place. They knew that despite what was going on around them, they would be loved and feel loved at the center. Many were kids I had known since I was a junior in high school, so it was a gift to be able to continue to work with them. They became a part of my greater family.

CHAPTER 5

A Crossing of Two Paths

The beginning of my sophomore year of college, I was determined NOT to date anyone. Up until that point, I was always interested in boys, but never really dated. I had gone on only a handful of dates in my life, but in all honesty, I would've rather just hung out with guys. I was a no-frills, no-drama, type of girl.

I accepted a position as a resident assistant (RA) and decided nothing was going to stand in the way of me growing in my relationship with God and investing in the girls on my floor of my dorm hall. I was on a spiritual high and no boy was going to get in MY way.

I should back up a little. A month prior to that decision, even though I wasn't interested in dating anyone, I had made a list of the type of guy I wanted to marry. It wasn't just any ole list that contained the typical "handsome, athletic, and Christian" characteristics. No, it was a list of 37 items of perfection. Of course, my #1 was that he had to be a Christian. Then from there the numbering wasn't as important, though in my mind, I wanted a spiritual leader, someone who wanted to be in some sort of ministry (preferably youth ministry), romantic, good listener, adventurous, cute smile, tall (6'3" or taller), liked sports, sincere, and the list went on. And on... (not that I was picky or anything).

Anyway, enough about that list – back to my sophomore year. The week before students were to arrive on campus, the RAs made their way through the dorm room hallways, praying for each student. One door on the guy's floor, below my floor said, "Dan Sterk."

That name rung a bell and, ironically, our paths had crossed before.

Let me stop here and tell you a bit more about this guy, Dan Sterk. His dad was in the Navy, serving on a submarine, until Dan was two years old. Dan was the youngest of three boys. After eight years in the Navy, his dad got out and they moved up to St. Joseph, Michigan, where his dad worked at a nuclear power plant, from which he has now retired. His mom went back to college to get her degree in music education.

Dan's upbringing was very similar to mine, though he was more of an "in the moment" type of guy. If he had the money, he would spend it. If it looked fun, even though it was dangerous, he would do it.

Although, Dan's experience with relationships was a little different than mine. To this day we have a disagreement on how many girls he dated, but he was a little more well-versed in the relationship department than I was. I make that point only because I was highly lacking in that area, which makes for an interesting story later on.

The summer after my freshman year of high school, I went with my friend's church down to St. Joseph/Benton Harbor,

Michigan, for their Youth Unlimited SERVE trip. These trips were designed to bring high school students from all over the United States to an area outside of their backyard and out of their comfort zone. The week was spent reaching out to the people of that community, while meeting people from all over the United States. Dan's dad and mom just so happened to be the ones in charge of leading that SERVE project.

So that summer on the mission trip, this handsome guy Dan, was the drummer for the worship band. Back then, I thought that any guy who had rhythm was already attractive by default, but then there was DAN. He was "that guy" every girl thought was hot stuff, but didn't ever dare speak a word to. We all thought he had a girlfriend, since there was this girl who always hung around him. Come to find out, that was only partially true. He had a girlfriend, but it wasn't the girl that was always hanging around him.

Fast forward to the summer after my senior year of high school. My friend Erin and I were supposed to go to Trenton, New Jersey on a two-week mission trip, but because of 9/11, the trip was cancelled. As we looked into other options, we decided to apply to the St. Joseph/Benton Harbor SERVE, since my first experience there was so life-changing. Our youth pastor called Dan's dad, who was still in charge of running that trip, to see if there was an opening for two girls; and there was.

That year though, Dan was a whitewater raft guide in South Carolina, so he wasn't at that SERVE, and obviously not the drummer. Meanwhile, it had only been a year and a half since my open heart surgery and I was still on various prescription medications. As the policy is with any type of camp, or over-night retreat with teens, you typically have to give the leaders all of your daily medications, so that they can monitor the taking of them. So I turned over my small personal pharmacy to Dan's mom, and every morning, I had to go to her to take my meds. That created the opportunity for me to get to know Dan's mom through conversations, mainly about being a tall woman since she is also 6'1".

I should add too that the summer before Dan transferred to Reformed Bible College, he had been casually dating, but had grown tired of dating without a purpose. One evening after coming home from a date, Dan sat on the edge of his parents' bed and engaged in a conversation with his mom about dating. He told her he was tired of dating different girls that he saw no future with. He told her the next girl he dated was going to be someone he could see himself marrying. He began to go over a list of qualities that this girl needed to have. First, she had to be a woman who desired God and be someone that he'd be proud to take home to his parents. Then the list from there became a little more light-hearted. She had to be adventurous, love the outdoors, and have a good sense of humor. Then the list became frivolous; rounding out the list, the next girl he dated had to be at least as tall as his mom.

Now, back again to my sophomore year of college, move-in day. As I was busy meeting and greeting the girls who would be living on my floor, I ran into a man holding a lamp. I immediately recognized him. It was Steve Sterk, Dan's dad, and he'd made up some excuse about ending up on the wrong floor while trying to help Dan move into his dorm room. How he ended up on the wrong floor I'm not sure because Dan's dorm was on the ground level floor. Clearly it wasn't an accidental run-in, but an intentional meeting to try and convince me to go down one floor and talk to his son.

Here was the problem: remember the pact I made with myself? I was supposed to take that year and focus on my relationship with God; NOT my relationship with boys. After a few hours of contemplating, I decided to accept the challenge. What would it hurt? I'm the type of girl who, if given a challenge, will accept and go full force.

Due to my lack of relationship experience, I knew I needed a wing woman. I had crushes on boys, but never had the guts to actually talk to them. I mean who does that? Talking to them was like asking me to skydive (and this girl is deathly afraid of heights). Even though I was a talkative person, when it came to boys, you could hardly pry my lips apart. I was as naïve as they come.

I asked a fellow RA if she'd be willing to come along with me so I could say I accepted the challenge from Steve. Knocking on Dan's door led to my body sweating in places I never knew it could, as I almost felt another heart problem coming on. To recall what we talked about would require me to get past my nerves to remember! Despite the nervous sweats, we apparently were able to have a decent conversation because it was the start of something in the making.

⌇♡⌇

Later that night, the all-college bonfire was the social event to attend. As a RA, I was required to attend as many social events as possible to get to know the girls on my floor. We all settled into our mingling groups around the fire, making small talk. It was every introvert's worst nightmare, while it was every extroverts thriving moment and believe it or not, I would consider myself an extroverted introvert. I can be outgoing at times, but then need to slide back to my own comforts after a while.

At one point, I remember looking up and glancing over to my right and seeing this tall, handsome, muscular man, making his way to the group I was standing in. With hands in his pockets, this guy made a t-shirt and baggy khaki shorts look mighty fine. By the end of the night, when most made their way to bed, Dan and I were left standing by the nothing-but-coals fire.

Lying in bed that night, my heart felt something it hadn't ever felt before. (So cliché to say, right)? I couldn't help but wonder, was this REALLY the start of a relationship? No way. I wasn't going to date anyone for the WHOLE school year, let alone start a relationship on move-in day!

There was something about this guy though. There was something that intrigued me. He was far different from the type of person I thought I would ever date. That is why I pushed the idea of this guy far off in the distance. Yet his demeanor, his gentle conversations, his questions, and his background, appealed to me.

I always pictured myself with a basketball player; someone who grew up in the area I did, and grew up just like I did. Basically a male clone of myself. Looking back, how boring, right?

Then I met Dan. He was this whitewater raft guide, who wasn't doing college the conventional way. He went to a community college for three years and left with 30 credits; essentially what your average student finishes in one year. He grew up near Benton Harbor, the area I grew to love, and was a little mischievous.

For instance, Dan and one of my guy friends decided to get some skunk spray and spray it by the resident director's door. Mind you, this was like the third day of school. You can imagine the stench that filled not only their apartment, but the whole dorm. People knew that I was hanging out with Dan and now he was known as the "skunk spray guy." Here this new guy on campus was already causing issues and I was a bit embarrassed, yet still intrigued.

You see, I was a rule follower. I never did anything to remotely break the law (except one time I did get pulled over because my license plate light was burned out – didn't even know I had one). Then in school, anything less than an A meant I could've done better.

And here I started to hang out with this guy who was already creating a name for himself as the troublemaker.

But then I made a mistake. I mean a BIG mistake. The type of mistake that will go down in infamy.

That move-in day weekend might be the most memorable for his family, yet the most embarrassing for me. On a quiet Sunday afternoon, I decided to venture down to the dorm lounge to see who all was relaxing and hanging out. Lo and behold, Dan and his brother Tom were playing pool. We ended up talking about their dad, Steve. I'm not sure how it led to this, but at one point I ended up calling Steve "dad," and after that, there was no turning back; damage done. Tom called his dad to tell him and I never heard the end of it.

Needless to say, we started to hang out more and more. We started off slow with walks around "the loop" on campus. It was what couples did; plus, it was great entertainment for everyone on campus because then they could easily spy through their windows as they watched relationships in the making.

Though the more time we spent together, the more I knew I had to tell him about my heart condition, but my nerves took over every time. Each time I thought about mentioning something, I feared Dan's response. I knew when I started to date someone seriously, I'd have to tell him what marrying me could mean. Was I really ready to deal with this reality?

36

After my heart surgery, the doctors were uncertain the repercussions my surgery would have on the rest of my life, since most didn't make it to 17 years of age.

My mitral valve was leaking prior to my surgery, but they thought it'd fix itself after surgery when my heart was properly plumbed. That wasn't the case. My heart was so damaged prior to surgery, that as time progressed, my doctor feared my heart wouldn't be able to handle a nine month pregnancy in the future. It was a repercussion that I had no reason to think about, until I realized I had to tell my future husband one day, what marrying me might mean. I feared that someone would choose to not date or marry me because of my inability to have children. Now here I was – wanting to date Dan.

Little did I know, classmates at college kept warning Dan, "Wait until you hear about her heart." Of course this "warning" sparked some curiosity in him because why would my heart be such a big deal?

One night, when the cafeteria wasn't serving dinner, I decided to make my own Easy Mac. Dan happened to call me after I already ate every college student's dream meal, to see if I wanted to go out for dinner. I of course said no, since I had already eaten and was oblivious to the fact that he was asking me out. So Dan hung up and I moved on.

Then Shaun, Dan's RA, called me and asked, "What were you thinking? You can't shut a guy down like that!"

Shaun and I had become good friends while being RAs together, so he had the right to call me out like that. Then bound and determined Dan, called again: "I know you already ate dinner, but I bet you haven't had dessert." I had not.

That night was our first official date. We went down the road to Applebee's, and grabbed that dessert Dan asked me to get with him. It didn't take long before he casually mentioned that people were telling him that he needed to ask me about my heart. After a comment like that, I knew it was time. I couldn't lie and say it was nothing.

Applebee's maybe wasn't the most opportune time considering the noisy atmosphere, but I knew I had to. As I began to tell my story, all those fears of how a guy would respond diminished as Dan accepted my story with grace, understanding, and love. This intriguing guy, had my heart.

As our relationship progressed, I knew God had chosen this man to be my husband. A man who saw my scars as a story about where I'd been, but didn't define me or determine where I was going in life. He often told me my scars made me more beautiful and THAT was the type of man I wanted to spend the rest of my life with.

Oh, and remember that list of 37 qualities I was looking for in my dream husband? Dan fit every single one of them. From a cute smile, to being in ministry (he was a youth ministry major), to being 6'3". Not to mention, he also liked sports and was adventurous. Goodness, he was a white water raft guide!

Fast forward two years. July 2005, I had driven to Dan's hometown, St. Joseph, Michigan, for a visit. Dan's mom invited me down so we could do a day away in Chicago with Dan's sister-in-law and his brother's fiancé. I drove down the night before, and immediately when I walked in, Dan seemed unusually talkative. Of course we were always excited to see each other, but that day in particular, the excitement level seemed to have risen.

We walked out to the backyard and sat down in the hammock where we caught up on each other's week, which wasn't out of the ordinary. I asked Dan what his week entailed and he nonchalantly said he went out for lunch with my dad. At the time I thought that to be very odd because Dan wasn't one to just "talk to my dad." Then he bluntly said, "I asked him if I could marry you."

I wasn't sure what to say and I'm sure my look of shock said it all. I looked at Dan and with all seriousness he said, "Well, will you?"

Dan is a no-frills type of guy. He is a say-it-how-it-is type dude. Sure enough, Dan reached into his pocket and pulled out the most beautiful ring; a simple ring that was completely me. The next few minutes were a bit of a blur, but I'm told I jumped out the hammock so fast I almost flipped Dan out of it. Apparently, I'd never even said yes, so Dan had to ask the question again. That time I was able to answer with a big ole YES.

He said he had ideas to propose on the beach while the sun was setting, but the fact that he couldn't wait, had the ring in his possession for a total of two hours, spent all he had to get it, made the proposal on the hammock that much more meaningful and beautiful. In fact, he even had to borrow money from his mom to pay for lunch when he took my dad out.

That was Dan's style, and still is to this day: spontaneous and live in the moment.

CHAPTER 6

When Two Become One

Spring of 2006, we both had just graduated college, bought a house a month prior, and Dan started a full-time job as a youth pastor. He also spent time working on our house so it'd be ready when I moved in after the wedding. Why not add one more big life event to the mix by getting married, right?

I was planning a beautiful spring, May 12 wedding, assuming we'd have mild temperatures. I now tell anybody getting married to not plan your wedding around the weather (even though we were having everything inside) because you just never know.

It was 39 degrees and rained the entire blissful day. No glorious spring pictures outside with fresh greens in the background. The night before, right before our rehearsal, a storm knocked out the power to half of the church; thankfully that changed for the wedding day.

Regardless, it was a beautiful day inside and that was all that mattered. It was the covenant we made between each other – a promise – that through thick and thin, we would stick it out together. That day we were surrounded by our beloved family and friends, so what more could we ask for? Thus began a lifetime of life, love, and memories together.

When Dan and I were first dating, we talked about our favorite Bible verses. It was one of those cliché questions Christians ask each other when they first start dating and a question that is eventually asked by any marriage counselor. We both were shocked when we heard each other say Psalm 121. I mean, there are 1,189 chapters in the Bible.[4]

When Dan was a whitewater raft guide down in South Carolina, every morning he woke up to beautiful mountains, as he looked out of his little hut, with nothing but a screen for a window. It was a trying time for him because his co-workers lived a lifestyle of drugs and drinking that he didn't want to get into. As a faith reminder, he nailed Psalm 121 over the doorframe of his hut to encourage himself to stay strong. Let me add too, the actual job of a whitewater raft guide would alone cause you to cling to those verses.

If you remember, that Psalm brought its own meaning in my life because it was the one my pastor read the night before my open heart surgery in 2001, five years prior.

The choice of a wedding passage was clear: Psalm 121. Most people choose verses on love, marriage, or how to care for each other; but we chose the one that had ministered strongly to both of us, even before we knew each other. God had used those verses to help us through difficult situations early in our lives, and now together. Now they became a blueprint for our life as a married couple. And Psalm 121 would continue to be a blueprint to help us navigate through trials we had no idea were in our future.

You often hear newlyweds talk about the 5-year plan. This "plan" often consists of buying a home, purchasing reliable vehicles, and becoming financially stable. Then it's time to start trying to conceive. Seems pretty simple, right? Yet over the years, I've come to realize the 5-year plan is far from normal for some. For us, when all we wanted was normal, all we got was the not-so-normal.

I was accepted into graduate school for social work, and I was ready. Even though I'd have to drive 1 ½ hours one way, three times a week to attend, it was an accelerated program, so I knew it'd be worth it.

Though, the summer after we got married, I felt this nudge. It was that same nudge I felt my junior year of high school to not play basketball.

I couldn't explain it. Here I was on the fast track to a great social work career, ready to rake in the dough. Yet this nudge became heavy; a nudge that told me I wasn't meant to go.

I decided to quit before I even started. It was something that was difficult to explain, especially since everyone expected me to have this successful social work career. I had to go against the grain and against what others expected of me. Sound familiar?

For my whole life, I felt like I was living to please others, which was my own doing. It was a life of fear. Fear of what others thought of me. Fear of what the real self would look like. Would I be accepted? Would I fit in? I was a people pleaser and would do anything to please; so much so, that I often felt this overwhelming guilt that I was never doing enough. Fear ran my life to the point that I was losing who I was. It was fear that caused me to ignore the nudge to quit basketball. I felt I would be letting so many people down because basketball was what I was expected to do. An expectation that I put on myself.

So here I was at a crossroad again. Choose to follow the nudge or do what was expected?

I didn't have a logical explanation as to why I wanted to quit before I started. I had started working part-time at a local Christian bookstore in town, but found myself really enjoying that instead. I had gone to school for four years, obtaining my Bachelor of Social Work and Bachelor of Bible/Theology degree, only to work at a Christian bookstore?

I am sure to many, it didn't make sense. I didn't even fully understand it myself.

Back to the 5-year plan. We did buy a home and we were working hard to pay off our school loans, but each year past the 5-year mark, we were consistently asked: "When are you going to have kids? Why don't you have kids? Kids are always at your house - why not have your own? You are going to love being parents!"

I didn't always have the heart to tell them that it would be risky to have my own children. As far as we were aware, I could conceive, but it was the stress on my heart from carrying a child for nine months that concerned the doctors. At this point, the doctors didn't know for sure what a pregnancy would do to my heart, but they had some serious, well-grounded concerns. My heart doctor had said when I wanted to start thinking about having kids, to have some further testing done, to get a better idea of where my heart was at. Though there was a chance we wouldn't get a definitive answer either way.

With Dan being a youth pastor, many assumed we'd have our own children because we loved teenagers. When the questions started to come about when and why not yet, they started to chisel away at my heart. Each question was a reminder that I wasn't "normal" and that parenthood just wasn't that easy for us to obtain.

How do you tell someone, "No we may not be able to have kids because..." or "I know we aren't parents, but we can't help it..." or "We would love to, but it's just not God's timing..." or even, "If you only knew the desires of our hearts..." How was I supposed to respond? Each question caused my heart to weep. Each question made me feel inadequate and insecure.

CHAPTER 7

Gray

No little girl grows up thinking that she won't be able to have her own child. At one or two years old, girls have a natural motherly instinct that kicks into full gear. Give any girl a doll, and she will immediately put it under her arm (even if it's upside down) and ask her mom for a snack for it. My mom has a picture of me feeding Cheerios to my stuffed teddy with the biggest smile on my face; a motherly instinct nurtured at a very young age. Growing up, a girl doesn't ever think about the ability to NOT have kids. Ask a little girl what she wants to be when she grows up, and some already know the job title: "Mom."

Our desire for children was much like everyone else's. A desire that seemed so easy to obtain, but the realities, all too real. I was almost 27 years old, 10 years after my open heart surgery, and we still had no plan or direction from God regarding children. Dan and I decided that it'd be wise to accept my doctor's offer to do some further testing to determine if childbearing was genuinely ever going to be a possibility.

The main problem up until that point wasn't my past heart condition, since that was fixed via surgery, but over the years, my mitral valve started leaking more and more. Like I said, carrying a child for nine months could possibly only make it worse. Even though my previous problem was fixed, my heart was much like a broken bone - once broken, the chances of it breaking again were greater. The heart muscle had been stretched to the extreme before surgery, so it was more likely to stretch again, causing more leakage and possible heart failure.

According to the American Heart Association, "Heart failure is a chronic, progressive condition in which the heart muscle is unable to pump enough blood through to meet the body's needs for blood and oxygen. Basically, the heart can't keep up with its workload."[5]

What part of that news was supposed to be easy or okay? Too often I would try to bandaid the pain of not having my own children by telling myself that it didn't really hurt. That it really wasn't that big of a deal. But each time I went through that cycle, the pain grew deeper and deeper as I pushed it further and further down. Dan knew going into our marriage that I might not be able to have kids, thanks to that Applebee's conversation, but it was a harsh reality for him too. His way of coping was to tell himself, "Well fine, I didn't want kids anyway." It was just the best way he knew. He figured that something can't hurt you if you never really wanted it in the first place.

Our calling to youth ministry was by no means a mistake. In fact, it was what helped us get through some of those times when the bandaid just didn't seem big enough. We often said we saw our youth group kids as our own and as part of our family and those kids knew full well that our door was always open. So open that they knew where our hidden key was (though you had to have the gift of height to reach it). Even though we embraced them with hugs, there was still a void.

In October 2010, we decided to pursue some further testing to get a better idea of whether my heart could handle a pregnancy. My doctor suggested a transesophageal echo (TEE), where a camera would be placed down the esophagus to get a clearer picture of my heart, to determine the exact severity of the leak in my mitral valve.

Would we finally be able to have our own biological children? But what if the answer was no? I started to go into self-pity mode, wondering why I had to have this testing done in the first place. In my mind, I was supposed to be able to get pregnant, have babies, and live happily ever after with no issues.

After looking at the results from the TEE, the doctor determined that my mitral valve leak was classified as moderately leaking, though heading towards severe, which meant my dream of becoming a mother seemed grim. The doctors didn't say I COULDN'T get pregnant, but suggested that it would be better if I also had a stress test to define how my heart reacts under stress, much like what a pregnancy would do.

We left the office that day with few answers and only more questions and confusion. Was it safe to get pregnant or not? Was it too risky? What were the risks?

That night, Dan prayed that God would just make it clear what type of kids we were supposed to have – biological, adopted, or just be content with claiming our youth group kids as our own. The thing was, I wasn't ready for any answer outside of being told biological kids.

After that frustrating TEE test with unclear answers, God was gently teaching me that I was putting my hope in something that wasn't secure. In something that wouldn't eternally stand, which was my body.

The next day, as I was cleaning our church's sanctuary (I was a custodian for a few years), I caught a glimpse of Dan and all I could do was run into his arms and cry. I had my own desires that I wanted so deeply. I just wanted them to be God's desires too, much like the desires I had to be this star basketball player. A desire that maybe wasn't God's.

The year prior, I had started a blog that was nothing special, but was a journal of what was going on in our life. Really, it was just factual events, which I suppose was pretty boring if you ask me. My older sister had started one and since we lived a little more than an hour from my family, I thought it would be a good way for them to keep tabs on us until we saw our families again. Anyway, I wrote in a blog post that day: "I DREAM for the day that the doctors tell me that I am healed."

When I made my dream known to the world, I secretly thought the day would come.

There was nothing I could do to heal my heart. Diet and exercise wouldn't clear up the issues. Congenital heart disease required a release of control. A release of my own desires to fix it my way and in my time. A release that required me to give it to the One who created me - the One who was my only source of hope and my only source of healing.

Two weeks after my TEE test in 2010, I had my scheduled stress test. We sat down with the doctor to discuss the results and she chose one word to describe my case: gray.

She went on to explain that with my case, it will probably never be a black and white answer - it will always be gray. With my heart history and where my heart was at that point, she didn't think I'd ever be given a 100% yes, go for it. She had some patients who had heart conditions, had babies, and had great pregnancies and deliveries. She also had other patients who had heart conditions who didn't have great pregnancies and experienced heart failure.

My mitral valve leakage was confirmed to still be moderate, heading toward the severe stage, which meant I was very close to another open heart surgery. On the positive side of the stress test, my mitral valve did not leak more during exercise, nor did my heart function decrease; but it was clear the valve wasn't heading in a good direction.

So what did "gray" mean for us moving forward?

Regarding pregnancy, gray meant I had a wider spectrum of risk. The smallest risk would be shortness of breath and bedrest during the pregnancy. The biggest risk? Heart failure or possibly death. If my heart function declined while pregnant, the baby would have to be taken early, to not only save my heart, but also to save my life. The hope would be to make it to 32 weeks gestation, but if I couldn't make it that long, what would we do? Were we ready to make those difficult and ethical decisions? Was it worth running the risk of needing open heart surgery right after giving birth? Was it worth the risk of possibly dying? Was it worth the desire to bring life into this world, only to lose one in the process?

We felt that since those questions were running through our minds it meant God was telling us to just wait. Waiting for what, we didn't know, but we felt we had to accept the inevitable: biological children just weren't in our future.

At the end of my meeting with the doctor, she recommended that we get a second opinion. I have a lot respect for a doctor who suggests that! My doctor had a colleague at the Mayo Clinic who she was willing to send my test results to for a second opinion. Going that route appealed to us since we wouldn't have to actually drive out there. Plus, Mayo is world renowned for their expertise.

Well, Mayo said the same thing. We could keep doing test after test in hopes of hearing what we wanted to; but in the end, we never would. It was just time to move on, we found ourselves grieving over what we couldn't have.

What I struggled with most was the fact that some people didn't understand why we wouldn't just TRY and have kids to see what would happen. But those people didn't have to live with the consequences of a pregnancy gone wrong. They didn't have to live with possible heart failure the rest of their life. They didn't have to think about the possibility of dying and leaving not only a husband, but also a newborn behind.

The wounds of being told a pregnancy would be risky and the questions regarding why we wouldn't just try, started turning into scars. Different scars than the physical ones I already had. This time they were emotional scars.

One night I confessed to Dan what my heart was having a hard time accepting: that maybe God didn't have any babies for us to take care of here on earth and he replied, "Well yes He does! He has babies for us - just not for us to care for in our home."

He was right. God had blessed us with nieces, nephews, and our youth group kids. I was just constantly looking past the blessings God had already given us.

Dan taught me to keep looking up and looking out. We weren't trying to shut the door on God and the possibility of a miracle, but we had to accept the situation God had us in. My heart was not getting better, but only worse, and we needed to move on.

So why not adoption? We had a lot of people ask, "If you can't have your own children, why not just adopt?"

Adoption is not the cure for infertility or the inability to have kids. I mean that in the most compassionate but honest way. Adopting a child wouldn't have cured our pain or my inability to carry children. For us, even though we thought (and still do) that adoption was a beautiful process and an answer to the brokenness in our world, it didn't mean that it was the right thing for us at that moment. We weren't closing the door, but we also didn't feel an open door either. As with all major life decisions, I feel a call from God is the key, and we just didn't feel called by God to adopt. Simple as that.

In fact, over the next year, we actually felt our desire for kids start to fade. It was something we couldn't explain, but we knew this too, was from the Lord.

CHAPTER 8

Renewed Hope

(BRENDA)

It was September 2010 and I was 48 years old when I believe the Holy Spirit put it on my heart to be a gestational carrier (surrogate) for my friend, Kristin. Kristin was a young woman in her late 20's who had a defective heart valve and was told by her doctors that it would be life threatening for her to get pregnant and bear a child. She and her husband, Dan, struggled with the reality that they may never have a biological child. They were often heavy on my heart and so I would pray. I prayed fervently and often for them, that God would give them peace and that they would be able to accept this disappointment as part of God's plan for their lives. It was while I was praying for them that the thought was placed on my heart that I could carry their baby for them. I smile. I laugh! What a silly idea! But, I would love to be pregnant with their child! I had three healthy pregnancies when I was in my 20's, I loved being pregnant then, and I was healthy now.

I found myself filling with excitement about the possibility. But still, it seemed ridiculous.

When my husband Tim came home from work, I told him about my "thought" of carrying a baby for Kristin. He thought I dreamed up a good one this time! We laughed and talked briefly about it. We didn't know if it was even possible because of my age and the fact that I was already in menopause. I had an appointment scheduled the next week for my yearly check-up. Tim gave his permission to discuss it with my doctor the next week. So I did.

At my appointment, Barbara, my nurse practitioner, asked if there was anything else I wished to discuss with her. Ok, here goes... she opened the door... so I said it. "I'm considering being a surrogate for my friend and her husband." Barbara is so great; she didn't even laugh. She smiled and told me she thought it was a wonderful idea. She gave me a phone number of a fertility clinic in Kalamazoo and recommended that I start there.

As soon as I got home, I called the clinic. They transferred me to their Grand Rapids office and I talked with Christine, their counselor. To start the process, I needed to send them all my health records, including my previous pregnancies and deliveries. No easy task considering my last baby was 20 years prior! Thankfully, my doctor's office was able to produce some records from the archives and I sent them to Grand Rapids. Christine cautioned me that the cut-off age for a surrogate was 48 years old. She also told me that what I wanted to do for Kristin and Dan was called a gestational carrier, since surrogacy in Michigan was illegal. So I scheduled an appointment with Dr. Young to see what he had to say. Sadly, they couldn't see me until early December. I was frustrated because my biological clock was ticking, I was nearing my 49th birthday, and I didn't have time to wait. But I must wait.

As I waited for the day of my appointment, I was so excited that I could hardly stand it. Tim and I talked about it in much greater detail. I discussed it with each of our kids and they were all for it! Two of them were in college and one graduated from college and now working. They thought it was kind of weird, but fully supportive. They each had a close relationship with Dan and Kristin as well, and they would love for them to have the opportunity to have biological children. So the excitement was building. Except for Tim. He had some reservations about it. After a phone call to our insurance company, we were told that I wouldn't be covered by insurance. Not the transferring of embryos, not the pregnancy care, not the delivery. That was a rather large obstacle for Tim. Not so much for me because I felt that if God wanted to do this for Dan and Kristin, then He would supply the resources and care somehow. But Tim was pretty adamant that he wouldn't allow this without insurance coverage. He did, however, encourage me to keep my appointment with Dr. Young at the Fertility Clinic in Grand Rapids.

The morning of December 13, the day of my appointment with Dr. Young, I awoke to lots of snow. During the night it had snowed several inches and it was still snowing and blowing. People were encouraged to stay off the roads. We lived 1 ½ hours from Grand Rapids and most of the drive was along Lake Michigan, which was often treacherous during the winter months. I had to cancel my appointment and reschedule for January 17. I was so disappointed. I didn't want to wait. My hopefulness began to dwindle. Maybe I heard wrong. Maybe this was a "Brenda thought" and not a Holy Spirit prompting. I continued to pray that God would show me the way and make it very clear if this was something to pursue.

On January 17, the weather was good, and I drove up to Grand Rapids to meet with the fertility doctor. After reviewing my medical records and discussing my health, my lifestyle and my reasons, he told me that he couldn't see any reason why I wouldn't be able to carry a child for Dan and Kristin. I asked if we needed to move quickly because of my age. Was there a cut-off point where he'd be unwilling to work with me? He said no, he thought I was very healthy and would be willing to work with Kristin and me. But first, he wanted me to meet with a high risk OB/GYN, then have a sonohysterogram to ensure that my uterus was healthy enough to carry a baby.

With each appointment there was fear. Fear that this appointment would be the thing that would close the door to this journey. But with each appointment, God didn't close the door. The high risk doctor was fully on board and the sonohysterogram showed that my uterus was healthy.

Ok. So now I know that it's a possibility. I have a doctor willing to work with me, Dan, and Kristin. Now I just needed to know for sure if it was God's will.

I was so excited about the possibility, but I had to wonder if this was Brenda trying to fix something or if it truly was God leading me to be a gestational carrier. So I continued to pray and wait. I wasn't sure what I was waiting for; maybe a sign, maybe confirmation, or maybe for this crazy idea to pass.

But it didn't pass. Tim and I talked about it so much that we could no longer discuss it. The issue of insurance was a big obstacle for Tim. He would never give his consent for me to carry a baby without insurance, pure and simple. But I wasn't going to give up the possibility yet. We couldn't talk about it, but I could still pray about it!

About that same time, Kristin had an appointment with her heart doctor. They ran tests to determine if her heart was getting worse and began discussions about another surgery. Her doctor also wanted to send her records to Mayo Clinic to see what they would suggest. I wondered if maybe Kristin might be able to carry a baby if she had the surgery. Maybe her heart would be strong enough after they made the correction. These were questions that needed answers, so more waiting. There were many unknowns yet with Kristin's heart and Tim wasn't changing his mind, so I continued to pray and wait on God.

After Kristin got all the results back from her tests and the recommendation from Mayo, her doctor concluded that her heart wasn't bad enough to require surgery yet, but also discouraged them from ever getting pregnant. This was hard for Dan and Kristin to accept. They tried so hard to be trusting in God's plan, yet they were hurting so badly. It seemed like now wasn't the time to have a conversation with them about having someone else *carry their baby for them. Plus, I continued to struggle with Tim's stance on it. I couldn't imagine God calling me to do this without the full support of Tim. Some doubt began to settle in. I was so confused. Why would God put this idea into my head if it was just going to end in a dead-end? Maybe I heard wrong. Maybe God didn't put the thought in my head. Maybe I just thought it up all on my own. Maybe it was just Brenda wanting to fix it. There were no more conversations about it; just silence.*

After many months, my oldest daughter asked me if I had ever talked with Kristin about my "wild idea." When I told her that I hadn't, she asked what was I waiting for. I explained that I believed God wouldn't ask me to do this without the full support of Tim. Since nothing about the process seemed to be covered by insurance, Tim couldn't support it. I told my daughter that I'd never speak to Kristin about it unless Tim came to me and suggested we move forward and talk to Dan and Kristin. That would be my sign.

Several months after that conversation, out of the blue, Tim came home from work and announced that he had an interesting conversation with someone from insurance that day. He was told that the pregnancy care and delivery would be covered by insurance. To make sure, he had them put it in writing. Then he said to me, "I think it's time to talk with Dan and Kristin." Wow. There it was. My fleece. By now a year had gone by. I was almost 50 years old, but I had renewed hope!

$$\rightsquigarrow\!\heartsuit\!\rightsquigarrow$$

After arriving home from work one night, I glanced at our answering machine and noticed we had a message from my dear friend and mentor, Brenda. She was wondering if she and her husband Tim could come over that night to run something by us. Even though it wasn't out of the ordinary for Dan and me to get together with them, we were still a little curious as to why they wanted to come over.

Before I continue, what you must know is that there was a lot of history between us and the Vriezemas. They'd been friends with Dan's parents for years, and Brenda was even Dan's Sunday school teacher when he was in preschool. After getting married to Dan, I too, had the privilege of getting to know Tim and Brenda. They welcomed me as one of their daughters and we became more than friends. We'd spend hours and hours talking because they were the type of friends that you could relate to on every level of life. We grew together spiritually while doing a weekly Bible study with a few other women. The Vriezemas were people we grew to trust, confide in, and had a deep spiritual connection with.

Back to that Monday night. When I first opened the door to let them in, my heart started to race because it just still seemed odd that BOTH of them wanted to talk, especially since it was after 9:00 at that point.

Laughter and joking began (as always), but I wanted to cut to the chase and get to the bottom of the meeting, so I awkwardly said, "So welcome..." in hopes that would deepen the conversation.

Tim and Brenda both began to tell us how they'd been praying for us regarding children and asked how we were doing with the reality of not having a biological child.

Then Tim asked, "Have you ever considered having someone be a gestational carrier for you?"

"And what if someone offered?"

"And what if that someone was sitting right here?"

"And it wasn't me?"

To be quite frank, I had never heard of a gestational carrier. Dan hemmed and hawed over it for a few seconds and said it was something we had thought about briefly, but could never ask anyone to do.

Tim then replied, "Well, what if that someone was sitting in this room?"

I didn't even know what Tim meant, but Dan caught on to what he was saying and jokingly replied, "Tim, you can't carry a baby!"

I clearly looked confused because Tim clarified, "Well, Brenda is capable."

Dan started to laugh and I was just speechless. As I finally grasped (and understood) what they had just offered, I realized this was a bit of a crazy offer. Okay, it was nuts.

I didn't doubt Brenda's ability, but how could I say yes? The word "undeserving" kept coming to mind. I had so many questions and doubts. Though every doubt or question I had about the feasibility of doing this, Tim and Brenda had an answer for. We didn't realize it when they first walked in the door, but they had a folder stuffed with information they had researched. They had already looked into whether insurance would cover Brenda once she became pregnant. They had looked into fertility clinics, and had even found an attorney that would help us jump through the legal hoops required for this.

If Brenda had come to us a year prior, which would've been soon after we found out we couldn't have our own children, we would've clung to the wrong hope yet again. Throughout that year, God showed me that my life was not my own – even my body. I couldn't put faith in my body because that too could fail; but my Heavenly Father, He wouldn't.

In that previous year while God was chiseling our own hearts, Brenda was cleared as the perfect candidate to be a gestational carrier.

As we continued to talk that evening about what this would mean, we all kept coming back to whether this was God's will or not. Tim and Brenda knew that God had led them this far. After our year of struggling with not having our own children, God was working on Tim and Brenda to use them as an answer to our prayers. They had answered the call on their life. It wasn't a quick decision on their part; in fact, it was a year in the making. Now it was up to us to determine if it was God's will for OUR life. Of course, everything in us wanted to say YES, but that would've been a rather abrupt decision.

After we finished joking around, talking about how crazy this idea was, yet how Tim and Brenda felt God leading them down this path, we ended the evening in prayer. Though the only words I had left were in the form of tears.

After they left, we held a folder full of papers possibly describing the next chapter of our lives. A chapter of possible parenthood and a story of God's undeniable grace, provision, and orchestration, through Tim and Brenda offering such a gift.

(BRENDA)

As we waited for their answer, we continued to pray for guidance, for peace, and for courage. I gave lots of thought to how I wanted Kristin to be able to participate in the pregnancy of their child, how they could bond with their child when he/she was in my womb. I was bursting with excitement and hoping I would have the opportunity to be used by God to bring a baby to Dan and Kristin.

A few days later, Dan called and asked if we would come over to discuss it with them some more. As they prayed over it and discussed it, many questions surfaced. Many of their questions were the very things I had been thinking about as well. God had given me several pictures in my mind of how they could participate in the pregnancy. One picture that stands out in my mind, was Dan, Kristin, and myself, sitting on the couch reading children's books to their baby in my womb so that the baby would be familiar with their voices and their touches. I imagined that we would be spending lots of time together. So we discussed these things and at the end of the conversation, Dan said they would like to move forward in the process. We were all so excited and filled with anticipation in watching God work out all the details.

One thing I thought about a lot was how I was going to give God all the glory when Dan and Kristin had their baby in their arms. I wanted to be able to share about the miraculous way God had worked. In November 2011, word began to get out about what we were pursuing. Most people were genuinely happy for all of us, while some were skeptical. But what I wasn't prepared for was the praise that I would receive for offering to be a gestational carrier. It was November 20, a Sunday, and everyone at church was talking about it, praising me for what I was doing. I tried to deflect the praise to God, but I felt as if I failed miserably. I felt totally misunderstood. I wanted everyone to know it was God, not me. All the glory that I wanted God to receive went straight to me. I robbed God of His glory. Already. I came home from church so disappointed in myself, feeling like such a failure and lousy person. After lunch, I read Jesus Calling by Sarah Young for that day. The very first words of that devotional read, "I am pleased with you, my child."[6] Those words stopped me. Those were the very words I needed to hear. I felt that I had let God down and He spoke His love to me, in spite of my failure. Wow. That day Tim and I discussed ways to deflect any personal praise to God and His goodness.

CHAPTER 9

A Humbling Offer

So let me put this in perspective. Someone offered to go to the doctor for over a year, get tests done, do research for us, pray endlessly for us to have a child, talk to their three children about a crazy idea, all without us knowing. Someone offered to carry our baby for nine months, go through the pains of labor, to only give that baby back to us as a gift?

After we accepted their offer, we knew that regardless of the outcome, our lives would never be the same. We didn't feel worthy or deserving, but knew this was all part of God's grand plan.

Though sometimes I had a hard time wrapping my mind around the idea of doing invitro fertilization (IVF). In order for Brenda to carry for us, an embryo would be created with my egg and Dan's sperm. When I thought about going through the IVF process, I was a bit scared, but also naïve. I knew some friends of mine had gone through it, so their friendship and encouragement were paramount. On the other hand, I was blogging, which in turn connected me to people from all over the country. I was (and still am) a pretty open book – or blog you could say. Some may think we are too open, but when I decided to talk about the gestational carrier process, it offered the opportunity to connect with others who had gone through not only IVF, but the struggle to have children.

Plus, blogging was a vulnerable journal for the world to read. You can share as much or as little as you want, by creating a picture of your life through simple words. I often found our life to be rather boring, but for some reason, I chose to keep blogging about it. Bless those who faithfully read every boring post.

Even though sharing about the carrier process made me a bit nervous about how people would respond, I inwardly hoped God would use our situation to encourage others to be vocal about what He was doing in their lives. But I also feared the critics. Those who maybe thought IVF was playing God. Those who thought we were going too far to have our own children. Again, I was letting fear get in the way of what God desired for our life and I was done living that way. This was our life.

We all have different chapters in each of our stories, but the same author: God. The chapters in your book look drastically different than ours, and they should. I personally find enjoyment in reading a variety of books. That is why it is important to let God write your story and not try to make your story like someone else's. We realized that God was writing a unique story for us and we couldn't help but share what He was doing.

Here is the story we shared with our family and friends, to let them know about the new chapter God was writing for our story:

Dear Family and Friends,

There is something that we would like to tell you all about, but we have been struggling with how and when to tell everyone. As many of you know, because of Kristin's heart, she is not able to carry a baby to full term. That has raised a lot of questions in our hearts and minds regarding family planning. We have thought about different routes and options, but we didn't have clear direction one way or another. Over this past year, as God has been working in our lives, bringing us contentment with the idea of not having kids, He has been working in Brenda Vriezema's heart. About a month and a half ago, Tim and Brenda approached us, wondering if we had ever thought about a gestational carrier (surrogate mother). That is something we felt we could never have asked someone and so we never even really considered that idea in the past. While talking with them one evening, they asked if we would consider having Brenda carry our child. We were speechless (still are). In the past month and a half, this is something we have been praying about, looking to God's leading for, to decipher if this is what He has planned for our life. We feel that this is an option that would glorify, exemplify, honor God's perfect plan, and how He brings brothers and sisters together in Christ through ways we'd never imagine.

At this point we have decided to pursue this, though we haven't started any of the medical procedures. We are currently in the process of working through the logistics. It is a lengthy and costly process with lots of legal hoops to jump through, but we are diving in head first. We don't know exactly when we are going to start the medical process of it, but this is something that has been consuming our lives and we do not feel we can keep it a secret from our dear friends anymore. It has been difficult to not share what God has been doing in our life, but we needed to make sure that this is what He was calling us to.

We would love to talk to you all in person, but we felt that by sending out a mass email, it was the best way to tell everyone at the same time. Also, this helps in making sure that everyone knows the same details. We do understand that not all of the details are covered, nor can we do that through an email like this. But this is something we are completely open and willing to talk about. In telling everyone this, we realize that it is no longer a secret. Our only fear is that as the news spreads like wildfire, people will think and assume Brenda is pregnant already. Let me clarify: she is not. We thank you for your prayers in the past and we covet your prayers for both us AND THE VRIEZEMAS as we proceed to follow God's will together. Though it would biologically be our child and Brenda would carry that child, we feel this is something that only GOD could orchestrate. We are only the instruments in His sovereign plan.

I never expected to find myself at a fertility clinic. I always thought I would have kids the "natural" way, but I quickly realized I was no different than anyone else in that clinic.

Fertility clinics have a stigma around them where only the really desperate people go to have children. The way I looked at it was if I was willing to go to the doctor if I was sick or to ensure my body was healthy, why wouldn't I go to a doctor when my body wasn't cooperating regarding my heart and having kids? Why was "infertility" seen as an issue that someone shouldn't go to the doctor for?

I also added my own stigmas and thought the mood in a fertility clinic would be depressing. I assumed like that of a regular doctor, it is a place you don't necessarily want to be. We experienced quite the contrary at our first appointment. At 8:30 in the morning, the woman at the front desk was overwhelmingly positive and cheerful. Clearly our expectations didn't include smiles and a genuine excitement coming from the other side of the desk. She offered a sense of hope and opportunity through her voice, which I needed to hear.

Meeting the fertility doctor, Dr. Dodds, for the first time was nerve-wracking; I think because we really didn't fully understand what we were getting ourselves into. Yet he was an optimistic man in a profession where success is not a guarantee.

Dr. Dodds went over all the procedures that needed to happen, the costs, where we stood with fertilizing embryos, and even talked about our faith. Because fertility is such an emotional, mental, physical, and even spiritual experience, it was relieving to hear him discuss his faith so openly as well. We felt understood, especially in a time when faith was the only thing we could hold onto. We knew God wasn't bound by statistics, so we were determined to not live by them either.

I think we would've started the medical side of things right then and there if we could have, but we had to meet a few more people and have some tests done before we could move forward. We quickly learned the concept of "one step at a time," since there was nothing quick about the IVF process.

An interesting and really befuddling aspect of the gestational carrier process was that we needed to legally adopt the child(ren) from Brenda. It seemed absurd at the time, but Michigan law stated that the person carrying the child was the mother, even if the embryo/child had no genetic ties to her. So even though the baby would purely be our flesh and blood, Brenda was still officially the mother. As a result of that law, we had to hire a lawyer to handle the adoption process.

Dan and I didn't know anything about acquiring a lawyer, but Tim and Brenda had given us a list of three lawyers in the state of Michigan who dealt with the gestational carrier process. Of course, lawyers are people you never really want to hire; but in our case, it was a positive reason. Plus, before we could start any of the procedures, we had to have a contract set up with Tim and Brenda.

While speaking with our doctor at that first appointment about the adoption process, he mentioned he knew of a good lawyer to use. We told him we had already talked to someone; ironically it was the same person our doctor was recommending! I don't know how many active lawyers there were in Michigan at the time who dealt with the gestational carrier process, but for us to be talking about the same one, that was only God.

Another open door.

After that initial appointment (and after almost every appointment), we went to Brenda's house to explain everything we had talked about. Each time we were filled with laughter, excitement, anticipation, giddiness, and hope.

That giddy laugh continued in our own house too. Dan and I would walk past each other and just start laughing. We'd be sitting on our couch and randomly say how crazy this all was and just laugh. We kept thinking about the story in the Bible in Genesis 17 and 18 of Abraham and Sarah who too laughed at the possibilities. They laughed at the craziness of what God said He would do in their lives, which was to have a child in their old age. Though as Jesus said in Matthew 19:26, "With man this is impossible, but with God all things are possible." God had answered our prayers in an impossible way, much like He did with Abraham and Sarah. We had been praying that God would answer the "BIG" prayers in our life and He sure did not disappoint.

Then Tim and Brenda asked if we had ever thought about having twins.

TWO? Twins were something we never could ask for (let alone ask someone to carry our child), so we honestly never even thought of it. Though after much prayer again, it became clear that we were to try for twins. It was a long and costly process, and by fertilizing two eggs, we were increasing the chances of it working. If only one took, great! If two took, great! Among the four of us, we decided it'd be completely in God's hands, just like any pregnancy; and by fertilizing two, we would be maximizing the opportunity God had given us.

There had been many times I wanted to just call Brenda to thank her repeatedly, but even a simple thank you just didn't do justice. Brenda was willing to sacrifice her time, body, and life, so we could have life. A gift that I still to this day want to repay, but no gift would ever be comparable.

When God takes you on an unexpected journey, He shows you things about Himself and His Word that may not have been clear before. The story of Zechariah and Elizabeth was brought to a whole new light when we saw ourselves relating to Elizabeth's struggle with barrenness. Ours was a struggle we didn't expect to deal with, but the Biblical account makes a whole lot more sense because of the journey God had us on.

Luke 1:6 says, "Both of them were righteous in the sight of God, observing all the Lord's commands and decrees blamelessly." It seems quite clear that they lived a very godly life, but their "blameless" living didn't mean their life was easy. The next verse says, "But they were childless because Elizabeth was not able to conceive, and they were both very old." Zechariah and Elizabeth were upright and enjoyed a clear conscience before God, but were infertile.

Let me insert here that we did not and do not live a blameless life, and therefore, are not Zechariah and Elizabeth. What I related to was the striving to live a godly life, yet struggling to have children.

Continuing in the story of Zechariah and Elizabeth: an angel appeared, unannounced to Zechariah. He told Zechariah that he was going to have a child. Like any natural human response, he was doubtful. As a result of his doubt, God took away his ability to speak for nine months because he didn't believe what the angel said. Now to be completely honest, I am thankful God didn't choose to take away my ability to speak when we doubted our future with children. God had every right to do so, to get His point across.

Then there is the story of Mary:

The interesting correlation between Mary and Elizabeth is that they are cousins and God gave them the gift of friendship. In fact, Mary went to visit Elizabeth for three months and at the time, Mary was pregnant, carrying the Savior of the world. Because of their friendship, they were able to experience their pregnancies together.

That was how I felt with Brenda. Even though I wasn't going to be the one carrying our children, but because of our close friendship, we were able to share the pregnancy together. The friendship between Mary and Elizabeth was so close that the baby in Elizabeth's womb (John the Baptist) leaped for joy when Mary entered her home. That was the same type of friendship Brenda and I wanted and desired: for those babies to leap anytime they heard our voices.

Much like Zechariah, Elizabeth, and Mary, there were countless questions we had to consider. What if the process didn't work? What if something happened to Brenda while she was pregnant? What about the babies? What if something happened to Dan and me while Brenda was pregnant, and we died? How many times were we willing to try? How are the costs going to be covered? When is enough, enough? How involved would we be in the pregnancy? What would the delivery room look like? Who would be there? What if we really did have twins? What would people say when they saw Brenda pregnant and knew she had grown children?

So many questions to answer, but the one answer we kept coming back to was this: God is God, and He would do what He pleased with us. That was when James 4:13-17 gave that reassurance, hope, comfort, and peace we needed to replace our doubt:

"Now listen, you who say, 'Today or tomorrow we will go to this or that city, spend a year there, carry on business and make money.' Why, you do not even know what will happen tomorrow. What is your life? You are a

mist that appears for a little while and then vanishes. Instead, you ought to say, 'If it's the Lord's will, we will live and do this or that.' As it is, you boast in your arrogant schemes. All such boasting is evil. If anyone, then, knows the good they ought to do and doesn't do it, it is sin for them."

Those verses were a reminder that we couldn't necessarily plan out every event, every situation, and every cost. If it was the Lord's will, God would see us through it all. There was no room for boasting or doubt because the process was out of our hands.

Those verses in James would be our roadmap for sanity. Before we knew what lay ahead, God prepared us to daily let go of the fears and let go of the worries and unknowns.

CHAPTER 10

Options

During one particular appointment at the fertility clinic, we discussed how many embryos to fertilize, but we already knew – two. When it came to creating embryos to use for IVF, we believed that every embryo created was a life, and needed to be given the opportunity to develop as a child. We didn't desire to have a huge family, maybe 2 or 3 children at the most. When going through IVF, to have the best chance of success, the thought is to create as many embryos as possible (typically between 6 to 8). This created a bit of a moral dilemma for us. If Brenda became pregnant with twins on the very first try, what would we do with the remaining embryos? At this point, the only options we knew were to keep them frozen forever, donate them to science where they would be destroyed, or dispose of them.

None of those options provided the opportunity for life, so we decided to only create two embryos. But as we were discussing our intentions with our fertility doctor, he asked if we had ever heard of embryo donation as an option. Never having heard of it, he went on to explain that at the time, there was a one-year waiting list at their clinic for people desiring to adopt embryos. They desired a child just like we did. Granted, our situation was a little different, but the emotions were still the same. These couples desired to have their own children, but were unable to conceive. For all we knew, we could conceive (though we had never tried), but couldn't go through a nine-month pregnancy. The issues were completely opposite, but the results were the same; neither of us could have children.

There was the option to freeze my eggs and fertilize as needed in the future, but the success rate was less than favorable. With only a 5% chance of having a take-home baby by going that route, we weren't sure that was the right choice.

This was the dilemma we encountered: we felt God saying to pay it forward through embryo donation, but we weren't willing to accept the challenge, but as our hearts started to ache with their pain, we realized we simply desired what everyone else at the fertility clinic desired, which was to experience a pregnancy. We too longed to announce that we were having a child. We dreamed of rocking a child to sleep at night. We knew the pain of not having dreams fulfilled.

Someone was willing to carry our child(ren) for us, so how could we in turn not offer another couple the same joy by allowing someone to adopt our embryos?

With the way God works, we knew He could possibly ask us to do some things that were out of the ordinary. The gestational carrier idea alone was a tad out of the ordinary, to say the least. God's call on both the Vriezemas and our lives felt so strong. I repeatedly told her that if it didn't work, we were CERTAIN that it was God's will, regardless. We had numerous people tell us that if

God had led us this far, why would He not follow through with giving us a child? Though that may be the most logical in the human sense, God didn't owe us anything. He could and would do whatever gave Himself the most glory.

As time progressed, we continued to wrestle with the question of whether or not to donate our embryos, if we created more than two. We had received a call from the doctor's office saying that if we were to go that route, I had to have genetic testing done to determine the probability of my congenital heart condition being passed on to our children. If there was a high risk of passing it on genetically, then we wouldn't be able to allow our embryos to be adopted by another couple; no couple would want to adopt embryos with known issues.

Of course, it was a few months' waiting list to see the genetic counselor. During that time, we still felt a little uneasy about the situation, but still felt God calling us to it; so we put out a "fleece." We prayed that through the genetic testing, that God would assure us of what He wanted us to do. We prayed that if God didn't want us to allow our embryos to be adopted, that the genetic testing would show there was too much of a risk in passing down my heart problem to our children; but if He did want us to go through with this, then let the tests come back showing little risk.

After going through the genetic testing, it was determined that my birth defect was multifactorial, which meant there were many factors (not just one gene) that caused my congenital heart condition.

The genetic counselor determined that there would only be a 3-5% chance our children would have any sort of heart defect, including anything outside of the congenital condition I had. The answer seemed clear.

One day, Dan was sitting in the woods hunting, reading through Scripture. God led him to 1 Samuel 1 where Hannah prayed and made a vow saying, "Lord Almighty, if you will only look on your servant's misery and remember me, and not forget your servant but give her a son, then I will give him to the Lord for all the days of his life, and no razor will ever be used on his head."

As Dan meditated on Hannah's prayer, he found himself praying the same prayer and making that same vow.

Even though it was an unsuccessful day for Dan in the woods as far as hunting, he spent that day sitting up against a tree with his head bowed, eyes closed, wrestling with God over and over about allowing our embryos to be adopted. Brenda had offered us the most amazing gift - the opportunity to have kids of our own - and now we had the opportunity to allow another couple to have the same joy.

Yet it was our uncomfortableness with the idea that was preventing us from doing so. We kept coming back to Hannah's prayer in 1 Samuel. Nowhere in Scripture has God ever said that His desire for us in following Him was supposed to be comfortable. We thought about what our denomination held as a doctrinal commentary to Scripture – the Heidelberg Catechism. In that Catechism, question and answer #1 says:[7]

Q: What is your only comfort in life and in death?

A: That I am not my own, but belong - body and soul, in life and in death - to my faithful Savior Jesus Christ...

There was our answer to being comfortable; our only comfort in life was that we belonged to God. So if we didn't even belong to ourselves, then how could we lay claim to any embryos we created?

Dan came home later that day and shared with me what he had been wrestling with. The thing was, I was having similar thoughts that day. It was evident that God was working on both of our hearts.

We had prayed for God to shut doors for nine months, but He kept flinging them wide open. We realized it was our selfish desires, fears, ignorance, and lack of faith that caused us to put up a wall and deny the call God was putting on our hearts. As we saw God opening doors, one by one, we felt we were meant to keep pursuing embryo donation.

Not only was our family size possibly growing, our life seemed to feel a bit like a whirlwind at times; especially on March 2, 2012.

For the past few years we had attended a youth ministry conference to regroup, refresh, and gain an incredible amount of new ideas, all while meeting fellow youth leaders and pastors who walked the same road of ministry we did.

That year, when we left for the conference in Louisville, Kentucky, we knew there were going to be storms, but didn't think much of it since it was March. Typically early March doesn't bear storms that are severe to us, except snowstorms.

75

As we were driving, we noticed the clouds were getting ugly. They were that greenish color my dad taught me about when I was a kid. Again, due to it only being March, we didn't think much of it, until we heard a tornado siren. Then we knew trouble was looming. We weren't exactly sure where we were, but we quickly turned on the radio and the first thing we heard was, "If you are in Scottsburg, seek cover immediately." We quickly glanced up and saw a water tower standing next to the highway that said, "Scottsburg."

We scanned the skies, but didn't see a tornado. With that said, I don't recommend that being the determining factor as to whether or not to seek shelter in a tornado warning. Dan decided to just floor it to get out of that town. As we continued to tune in to the radio, we heard the broadcaster say that a tornado had just passed through Scottsburg. We both looked at each other with sheer shock; we had just beaten it. Meanwhile, I was also texting my friend Sheryl, who was giving us weather updates, since this was prior to us having smartphones. Then we lost cell phone reception.

Within about 10 minutes, we heard again on the radio that there was another tornado just in front of us. At that point there was no exit to get off, so we just continued to drive. Our hearts started to beat a little faster, wondering what was lurking up ahead.

The next exit was Henryville, Indiana. As we drove up to that exit, traffic was at a complete standstill. Cars were turned every which way in the median. A semi-trailer was picked up and turned over the guardrail. Trees were slashed in half. Cars were dismantled. A tornado had just passed through. As we sat and waited for the traffic to start moving again, I glanced to my right and saw this massive dark black cloud. Remembering again the days of standing in the garage with my dad on the farm watching storm clouds roll in, I knew this was going to get nasty. Dan quickly grabbed the camera so we could get a picture of it.

Then that massive cloud started to grow darker and head our direction. As it got closer to us, additional sinister looking clouds began to collide with the original cloud in a choreographed chaos like a cat fight on the barn floor. The combination of clouds started chucking baseball-sized hail at us as we sat helplessly on the side of the highway. Hail bounced off the hood of our SUV and Dan jokingly said, "Whoa, I think that left a mark," but then the joking stopped. This was starting to get serious.

A hailstone sheared off the driver's side rearview mirror; that was going to be a little harder to fix. As the intensity of the hail started to pick up, we had to yell just to be heard, even though we were sitting right next to each other. The hail sounded like an army of junior high kids beating the bajeebers out of our vehicle with baseball bats. Suddenly we felt a draft of wind come rushing in from the back of our vehicle. A large hailstone had smashed through one of our back windows.

Looking out through the glass in our sunroof, we started to wonder how long that would hold. Not knowing what else to do, Dan closed the fabric sunshade to the sunroof. At least that way maybe we wouldn't have to see it coming. We never heard it shatter due to the deafening sound of the hail hitting our vehicle, but the tiny shards of glass raining down on us from above told us exactly what had happened; the sunroof had given way. Moments later, another large hailstone came smashing through the passenger side window and struck me in the calf like a major league pitcher hitting a batter who was crowding home plate. I tried to climb into the backseat to avoid the combination of glass shards and hailstones that came swarming in through the new opening, but Dan told me to stay put and keep my seatbelt on in case the tornado lifted our vehicle off the ground. At the same time, he grabbed a pillow from the back seat,

77

shoved it where my window used to be, and draped a coat over me to offer some shelter from the broken glass.

Dan was completely calm as I just shouted to God in desperation to spare our lives. What seemed like hours later (though it was just a few minutes), the hail stopped. The rain stopped. The wind stopped.

We stepped out of our vehicle to the sounds of screaming and complete chaos. We assessed the damage and realized with desperation, but also with relief in our voices, that God had spared our lives.

As we surveyed the area around us, it looked like a war zone. In total, we had lost three windows and the body of our vehicle looked like craters covering the surface of the moon. The ground was littered with giant hailstones, like a driving range at a golf course before the balls are collected.

We knew our vehicle still ran, even though it was a complete wreck, and the best thing we could do was get out of the area to make room for emergency vehicles that were coming our way. Other than a giant egg-shaped lump on my leg and a few minor nicks from broken glass, we were okay and didn't need any medical attention.

Dan once again put the pedal to the metal and wove through the tangled mess of battered cars along the highway, as we drove the last 20 miles to Louisville.

We arrived at the hotel downtown and everything seemed normal. People were out walking around on the streets, oblivious to the tornadoes that had just ransacked the area just north of Louisville. Dan told me to stay by our vehicle as he checked to see where we had to go for the conference, since our missing windows left us open to someone taking our belongings. When I watched Dan walk into the hotel, I panicked. It finally hit me that we were not okay. We had glass everywhere on our bodies and in our hair. Our clothes were soaking wet, and our vehicle was absolutely destroyed.

We drove into the parking garage and immediately a few people came over to ask if we needed anything as they stared at our vehicle in shock. I think they assumed our vehicle had been broken into.

Dan called the insurance company and how gracious they were. We thought it was kind of a strange claim to make, that a tornado had destroyed our vehicle, but they told us to take our time and that they would start to work on a claim. We offered to send them pictures for proof, but they believed us since it had already hit the news headlines, even in Michigan.

Meanwhile, a youth ministry icon in our world, Walt Mueller, who we had met at a conference a few years back, saw us as we were checking in. He pulled us aside and asked, "Are you guys okay?" As we just stared at him, he said, "You look like a deer in headlights." We thought we were fine, but I think he knew that we really were not.

After trying to figure out what to do with our vehicle, we went back into the hotel where we again ran into Walt. He had generously organized a room upgrade for us, free of charge. Something completely unexpected. So, we headed up to our now suite room, with tiny shards of glass still in our hair, clothes, and luggage. We called our families back home, starting the conversation with, "I'm not sure if you saw anything on the news, but we just went through a tornado, and we are okay." About that same time, we realized that we had left Sheryl, the friend who was giving us weather updates, hanging. So we quickly called her to let her know what had happened.

We turned on the evening news before going down to the mainstage and there it was - footage of the tornado that went through Henryville. Lives were lost, homes were a complete loss, and there we sat in a hotel suite. At that moment we realized how blessed we were to be alive. We clearly weren't at the center of the tornado, but oh to think of what could've been.

After posting some pictures on Facebook of the storm and the damage done to our vehicle, our friends, Adam and Lindsey, who lived in Columbus, Ohio at the time, offered to make the three-hour drive down to Louisville to help. They came armed with supplies to help clean out the pieces of glass that had rained down on us, and had clear plastic sheets to cover our shattered windows. What a gift and relief that was, since we really weren't sure how we were going to drive our demo-derby worthy vehicle the five hours back home.

Dan and I continued to attend the conference and soon became known as the "tornado" people. People would come up to us in the hallways and comment, "Hey, you were the people who went through that tornado!" Yes, we were those people and that was a story we told for months after.

We drove our vehicle home, thanks to the help of our friends from Ohio. It was a very chilly ride though, since it was snowing and three of our windows were shattered. We drove by the Henryville exit and there was much more damage than we remembered. I couldn't help but cry tears of relief, but also grieve for those who lost their lives.

We managed to get our vehicle to the body shop in our hometown and they showed us parts that were designed to not dent, like the roll cage. They stood in awe, looking at us, wondering how we were alive. Needless to say, our vehicle was totaled.

It goes without saying that the start of 2012 was an interesting one for us. We were in the process of starting to prepare for IVF and we had just survived a tornado. It was a lot to take in, in just a few short months, but it was all in preparation for our future. It was just the beginning of the storm to come.

Back to the gestational carrier process. I was clueless about how intricate the IVF process was. Before, I just saw it as a few more steps outside of the natural conceiving way. I had no clue that IVF was so intense and that I'd be creating a chemistry lab in our spare room every night. In fact, on July 29, 2012, I finally started the shots to stimulate my ovaries to produce more viable eggs. That afternoon, I injected my first dose of Lupron into my lower abdomen. I had to psyche myself up, but it was a piece of cake. With frosting! I felt only minor side effects, with the worst being hot flashes.

The time had finally come for me to have my first ultrasound. Not of a baby, but of how many eggs my body was producing. Those ultrasounds were a glimpse into what it would be like to see a baby inside of me. Of course, we prayed that one day we would see two little embryos inside of Brenda, but for those few weeks, I was able to experience what it was like to go in for ultrasound checks as a "pregnant" mama with eggs. I put my hand on them thinking that one day those eggs could possibly be our little children.

Unfortunately, in a later ultrasound, they found only five good eggs and two small ones. We were extremely disappointed and wondered if a successful egg retrieval would even happen. My nurse said that five good eggs was a low number, but those eggs looked good. We knew that medical technology would and could only go so far and that nothing could replace God. We had to leave the results in His hands.

CHAPTER 11

When the Rubber Meets the Road

Fertility issues aren't able to be solved in one day. For anyone who has struggled with having their own children, you know there are no easy answers. I didn't realize it at the time, but my fertility journey started the day I found out I might not be able to have my own children, 10 years prior.

We wouldn't know anything about embryo donation if we had children of our own the natural way. If we didn't know about it, we wouldn't feel the hurt for those who couldn't conceive. We wouldn't have met people who adopted embryos and eventually had successful pregnancies with those embryos.

Our desire was to obey God, which we felt was to give another family the same opportunity we had. We couldn't explain it and we didn't always understand, but the tug was so strong. Hebrews 11:1 says, "Now faith is being sure of what we hope for and certain of what we do not see." We were certain that if we weren't meant to do it, that God would change our hearts and close doors. At that point, He had yet to do so.

What we didn't expect, was to experience opposition about our desire to do embryo donation. God knew we were going to experience opposition, but would we withstand the test? Were we going to give in? Were we going to cave when things became difficult?

Unfortunately, the place we received the most opposition from regarding embryo donation was our local church. It was also the place of Dan's employment as a youth pastor.

When it came to the church, we were asked some really difficult questions that we weren't sure were fair to ask, such as, "If the embryos were born children, would we give them up? If we were able to have children on our own, would we still donate embryos? If we implanted all of our embryos, would we make more to donate?" Those questions were hard to answer because we weren't in those specific situations.

It became very difficult and draining to try and have answers for the different scenarios people presented to us. If we had the answers, there would be no need for faith. Faith was the very thing that God, from the beginning, had called us to use; not our own understanding. No matter how hard we tried to answer those questions, we felt our words were never good enough.

Those who questioned us weren't in our shoes. We felt that until someone walked the path God had chosen for us, had the same conversations with God we had, would they be able to answer those questions with the "right" answers?

One morning as I was getting ready for work, I was struggling. Not just a woke-up-on-the-wrong-side-of-the-bed struggling, but it was something much deeper. I was hurt, frustrated, and confused. I turned on the radio for something to maybe influence me in a positive direction. Well, God had set up a divine appointment to have me listen to "Turning Point" by David Jeremiah, an episode titled "Abraham: The Progress of Faith." I had never listened to David Jeremiah before, but I knew we sold his books at the bookstore I worked at, so I thought I would listen to what he had to say.

The broadcast was about how the faith of Abraham was an example for us today, calling us to submit to God in obedience, even when God called him to sacrifice his only son, Isaac.

My tears hit the floor. God knew my frustration, pain, and the opposition we were facing, and this was how He chose to respond. After hearing that broadcast, I realized I had SO MUCH MORE I needed to be willing to give and surrender to Him. I knew God was calling us to allow our embryos to be adopted, but God was also calling us to do it willingly. Not only should we be willing to give up our embryos, but we also should be willing to give up everything for Him, even when it didn't make any logical or human sense.

Abraham walked with such obedience, and because of that obedience, God blessed a whole nation; all because Abraham was willing to give up his only son. In thinking about doing that, we didn't want to make a mistake. If we didn't listen, if we didn't obey, who would suffer because of our disobedience? What blessings would others miss out on if we didn't obey? What blessings would we miss out on if we didn't allow our embryos to be adopted? We wanted to be willing to walk for days up a mountain like Abraham, with our only son, to sacrifice what God was calling us to give up.

Though, if we decided to do embryo donation, there was a possibility the IVF/gestational carrier process could end up not working. We wouldn't have a child of our own, and someone else that had adopted our embryos would end up raising a child that was biologically ours. I didn't understand why God would even make that a possibility, but I had to obey.

Amidst our uncomfortableness with embryo donation, we felt there certainly had to be some scholarly Biblical advice out there, so we went to see what our church denomination had to say about it. Our church's denomination published a report on bioscience and genetic engineering in 2003 and one of the guidelines for pastoral advice concerning life issues was:

"We must not recommend rules that bind the conscience in disputable matters. To do so would violate personal Christian liberty. Instead, we should prescribe only where God's will is clear. Scripture is clear that every human being is created in the image of God and is precious to God."[8]

We felt God's will for our lives was clear, yet we felt so bound. The pastor and elders in our church felt that creating more embryos than what we possibly intended to implant in Brenda, and allowing our embryos to be adopted, was unbiblical. We had spent so much time in Scripture, trying to discern God's will in this situation, and were a little surprised when they told us it was unbiblical to allow our embryos to be adopted.

When we pushed back a little and asked where that was in the Bible, we were told they couldn't give us a specific verse, but to trust them that it was in there. We were thinking maybe we missed something, so Dan sought out the wisdom of a previous pastor of his who he respected. In that pastor's humble opinion, he felt that our current church leadership was looking for something in Scripture that wasn't there.

Dan was blessed to have been meeting with one of the elders of the church at the time as well. Over the past few months, on occasion he'd ask if we had thought more about embryo donation. Little did he know it was actually something that consumed our minds and consumed our prayer life. We learned quickly that they were against it, but what did that mean for us? Even though we were open about our struggles and wrestled with the idea, in the end, we felt it was a family decision, and found it strange that Dan could be fired over something such as this.

Eventually the council wrote a letter to us, stating that they couldn't stand behind us in the decision. Though, we weren't sure what "stand behind" meant - did it mean they were formally stating they were uncomfortable with the idea? Well, we were too, initially. Did it mean that any children we had couldn't be baptized in the church and become a part of the church? We needed some clarification.

When we were given that letter, they said that if we had any questions, to call them. So Dan called one of the elders and asked him to clarify what "stand behind" meant. He wasn't able to give Dan an answer at the time, but promised he'd get back to us.

A week later, Dan was asked to meet with the elder that had given us the letter, along with another elder in the church, to clarify what "stand behind" meant. They stated that if we continued to go through with allowing our embryos to be adopted, Dan's employment at the church would be terminated. Granted, we had seen signs of this coming, but we were still naïve to think that Dan would be fired over something such as this. We didn't have any intention of changing our minds, so Dan asked when his employment would be terminated. The elders replied that they didn't figure that out yet, but that they were aware of the timeline of our gestational carrier process.

That left Dan and me to weigh our options. Did we truly feel God was calling us to allow our embryos to be adopted? Did we feel strong enough about it that we were willing to have Dan lose his job over it? When God calls us to follow Him, He never promises it will be easy. But was following the call worth it?

That night, we sat on the couch in our living room in tears, as we realized we were going to be forced to give up the church home Dan had grown up in, along with all of the youth group kids we had grown to love and view as our own. We realized we'd have to sell our home, since we couldn't afford to pay the mortgage on my part-time income. Also, if we were going to stay in youth ministry, we knew we would probably have to move away from family.

So many questions. The cost to follow God's will for our lives wasn't going to be easy. It would've been MUCH easier just to cave and follow human desires and not God's. It sure would've saved us a whole heap of trouble, hurts, and frustrations.

In the meantime, congregation members visited to share their thoughts. Some came with a loving and gracious heart, while others came spewing condemnation, telling us we were being defiant to the church authority. Words that cut incredibly deep and left me weeping. I had never felt so much hatred towards me and all I could wonder was, God is THIS really what you had planned for us?

At this point, we were one week away from the egg retrieval. When we shared the news that I had five good eggs for retrieval, instead of rejoicing with us, we felt shame and condemnation from our church. This was supposed to be an exciting time, but our church believed we weren't able to hear the voice of God.

Was this really true? Now our personal faith in God was being put into question. We longed to feel love, grace, and understanding, but that wasn't the case.

CHAPTER 12

A Fleece in the Form of Flat Tires

Even though it was ultimately our decision how many embryos to create, it affected Tim and Brenda as well. When we started the gestational carrier process, it was going to be a one-time deal. The number of embryos to be created was two. Brenda knew those babies were never going to be hers and had no desire to raise more children, but they offered this option as a one-time process.

With us questioning whether to create more embryos than two, it put Tim and Brenda in a tough position. They were uncomfortable with the idea, but were willing to put aside their thoughts and allow us to follow where we felt God calling us. It was while they were vacationing that the church had informed us all of their stance via a document that explained their position on embryo donation and adoption. The church leadership felt that if we went through with it, we would be living in unrepentant sin.

Tim and Brenda prayed fervently for God to make it clear. Even though they believed it was our decision, they were now involved; because they were members of the church as well, it affected them on many levels. When their vacation was over, they prayed that if we weren't meant to participate in embryo donation, that God would make it clear in a drastic way. They prayed that God would give them a flat tire on the four-hour drive home (now that's a bold prayer).

They experienced two.

(BRENDA)

In the days following our return home, there was so much turmoil. Suddenly, the joy in the gestational carrier journey was gone. I found myself frustrated and confused. I began to feel angry. Angry with our elders and pastor. Angry with Dan and Kristin. This whole journey was supposed to be about them having a biological baby, not others having their biological children. I wrestled between two thoughts: this was an obstacle placed there by the evil one and we just needed to stand firm and persevere; or this was an obstacle placed by God and He was trying to re-route us. Tim and I prayed and prayed, but no clear answer came.

We hated the upheaval this created at church. We felt stuck in the middle somehow. We began to fear that maybe we would have to leave our church family because of this process. We began to consider the potential loss to ourselves. Our intense personal struggle brought us to share our feelings with Dan and Kristin. We met with them to clarify our position more strongly. Our desire was to create two embryos and transfer them to myself and harvest more eggs and fertilize those, if pregnancy wasn't achieved in the first try. It was then that we learned that there was to be only one harvest of Kristin's eggs.

That new piece of information caused us even more conflict, pain, and doubt of our own position. However, in the end, we remained convinced that we couldn't be a part of something that violated our own moral conscience. No matter how much we tried, we couldn't feel good about being a part of a process that would create additional embryos for other couples to adopt.

Though we felt as if we were manipulating Dan and Kristin somehow. We felt as if we were preventing them from following through with something they believed God was calling them to do. We hated the place we found ourselves in. The excitement we once experienced was replaced with frustration and confusion and pain. This wasn't how I had envisioned it. I encouraged Dan and Kristin to just focus on our gift to them and let go of blessing other couples.

The day came when I had to take the "trigger shot" called HCG, in preparation for my egg retrieval. The timing of the shot was vital because it kicked the eggs into final maturation. If given too early, the eggs might not be mature enough, but if too late, the eggs could be too old and not fertilize. That meant I had to have it administered at 10:00 p.m. on the dot.

Typically, that wouldn't have been a problem, but we had planned to go to the off-road races at the fair that night, a little over an hour away. It was a place I had gone since I was a kid and I was bound and determined to not let the tradition die. Administering the shot would be the difficult part, considering it had to be given in the ole rear end. I couldn't inject it myself as I had done with my other shots in the abdomen.

Dan was pretty sure he could do it, but I wasn't okay with "pretty sure." Dan's fears in life could be summed up with three s's – shots, snakes, and sharks. Needless to say, I didn't want someone, who was fearful of shots himself, to administer a shot that would determine whether or not my eggs would reach the final maturation process. Kind of a costly mistake if not given correctly!

Ironically, one of the friends we invited to go with us to the off-road races was a physician's assistant. Talk about God working out every detail. Since giving shots in the rear was something she had done before, I was pretty certain she'd be the better bet.

While at the races, I think I asked Dan about a hundred times if it was time yet. Of course, we ended up being on the road when the clock dinged 10:00 p.m. We had no choice but to pull off the highway; my friend and I jumped out of the vehicle and bam, shot in the rear. It might not have been the most likely of places to give such a shot, but it had to be done at that exact time. Fortunately, there were no other cars on the highway at that moment! Can you imagine the thoughts running through people's heads if somebody had driven past? There I was with my backside exposed on the side of the highway, illuminated by the dim dome light in the car, and my friend sticking a needle in me. After we jumped back in the car, through laughter we said, "Did we really just do that on the side of the highway?"

On Thursday, August 23, 2012, the day of my egg retrieval, it was no mistake that I read the daily devotional, *Jesus Calling* by Sarah Young:

Entrust your loved ones to me; Release them into My protective care. They are much safer with Me than in your clinging hands. If you let a loved one become an idol in your heart, you endanger that one – as well as yourself. Remember the extreme measures I used with Abraham and Isaac. I took Isaac to the very point of death to free Abraham from son-worship. Both Abraham and Isaac suffered terribly because of the father's undisciplined emotions. I detest idolatry, even in the form of parental love.

When you release loved ones to Me, you are free to cling to My hand. As you entrust others into My care, I am free to shower blessings on them. My presence will go with them wherever they go; and I will give them rest. This same Presence stays with you, as you relax and place your trust in Me. Watch and see what I will do.[9]

On this very day, doctors were set to fertilize two of my eggs. In the end, after all of the chaos surrounding the decision of how many eggs to fertilize, we decided to just do two and felt peace about that decision. Day after day we prayed that God would just show us His will and we felt that after talking at length with Tim and Brenda prior to my egg retrieval, and hearing about their flat tires, we knew that was the fleece we had been praying for. It was probably one of the hardest decisions we ever had to make, especially since we felt God saying "Yes, do it," for so long! But then God answered our prayers in the form of two flat tires. That was our answer. Two. Yes, we started this process knowing we would create only two, but then God introduced to us the idea of embryo adoption. It was not a mistake, even though in the end we did not end up doing it. And even though it was a very trying time, we are to this day, grateful for the way God opened our eyes to other families who struggle with infertility and the different avenues families are created.

Two years prior, while going through various heart tests to see if my heart could handle a pregnancy, I was clinging to the hope that just maybe we'd have our own child someday. Now here we were, ready to retrieve and fertilize my eggs. Though after reading the devotional by Sarah Young, we were reminded that regardless of the outcome, I couldn't put our future babies above God. They were God's. As much as we desired to hold two in our physical arms, we had to release them to God and watch and see what He would do, just like Abraham released Isaac to the Lord.

The retrieval was rather painful, and to our surprise they found eight eggs, with only one being immature (which is expected). Doctors chose the best two and attempted to fertilize them.

Now it was time to wait and see what God would do. Would He choose to fertilize the two eggs the doctor chose? If He chose no, then we needed to understand that He was doing that for our own good and for the furthering of His Name. If He chose yes, then we needed to understand that He was doing it for the very same reasons. Either way, we knew God would do what was best.

The next morning I received a call that the two eggs they chose had indeed *fertilized*! For the first time, there were two little Dans and Kristins in this world, just hanging out at the fertility clinic.

I immediately cried.

(BRENDA)

By this time our enthusiasm had returned and we were all flying high by the time the day had come. I was so excited and so thankful because I just knew God was going to do this! At 50 years old, I would be carrying at least one baby for Dan and Kristin, possibly two!

Two days after the retrieval, our embryos were implanted into Brenda. At 10:36 that morning, I received this text from Brenda:

Dear Dan and Kristin, Your two babies are tucked away safely in me, taking residence with Jesus who also lives in me.

Tears welled up in my eyes knowing our two little embryos were nestled safe inside her womb and safe in God's hands. We were already overwhelmed that God would give them to us for even just those past 24 hours, but it was even more surreal to think we had two embryos in another person, in the same town, and just a few minutes down the road.

The next 12 days would prove to be crucial. We prayed and prayed that they would continue to find residence in Brenda's womb and continue to develop.

(BRENDA)

I felt my faith being stretched. Would God really do this? This was a time of deep contemplation for me. I found myself praying continually for those embryos within my body, thanking God for this privilege. He gave me songs that spoke to my heart and carried me through to the day of the pregnancy test.

While we waited to see what God would do with our babies in Brenda, the struggles at the church came to a head. I should say too, in sharing about the opposition we faced, we aren't trying to dispute the position that our church stood for. How the church leadership handled the situation was how they sincerely believed was correct. These are our feelings and recollections during that difficult time in our life. We obviously hope that the church continues to move forward in its ministry with a loving and unified spirit, for the benefit of God's kingdom, and for the good of its members.

Because of the backlash from our church, we were scared we would say something that'd be taken the wrong way. I then found myself viewing God the same way, fearing I would say something wrong to God. I was living in so much fear that I felt I had to word my thoughts just right to Him so that He would understand. We felt little grace from our church and felt our worth was defined by whether we agreed with the elders and pastor or not.

At the end of August, after we created only two embryos, Dan had a meeting with two of the church elders. They informed him that his employment was being suspended indefinitely. He wasn't to have any contact with youth group kids or their families, but was allowed to come to church Sunday mornings. This was very confusing to us since we had done what they had asked us to do in creating two embryos.

There was this sense of control that felt so binding in all of this. When they said we were "allowed" to come to church on Sundays, it felt constraining, especially since we weren't to have any contact with youth group kids and their families. So without being allowed to give a reason or explanation, Dan quickly cancelled all youth group events, but had to pretend everything was okay.

A week later, on September 5, which also happened to be the same day we would find out if Brenda was pregnant, Dan was informed that his employment with the church was terminated as of that morning. The most hurtful part was that at a previous meeting, we were told that they knew of our timeline, so why choose to fire

Dan on the same day we were going to find out if Brenda was pregnant? It just felt like one more dagger. After seven years of employment there, it was over, just like that. For the past month, after being told that he'd be fired if we didn't follow the church leadership's desires, Dan had been going into work every day, wondering if it would be his last day. I suppose at least now we had the answer.

At the time of Dan's termination, he was given a separation agreement that he had to sign within 48 hours if he wanted to benefit from a three-month severance package they were offering. In that agreement, he had to promise to be amicable in the separation and not dispute the position of the church regarding his termination and defer all questions of his separation to the elders.

When he came home after that meeting and shared with me that he had lost his job, we realized that we had no other choice but to sign the agreement since we had just spent our entire life savings, and then some, on the gestational carrier process. We had nothing left in the bank to live on and still had more bills coming in.

So with reluctance, Dan signed the separation agreement, buying us some time to figure out what we were going to do next.

CHAPTER 13

Knitted Together

The day before we were to find out if Brenda was pregnant, I told her that either we'd be walking the road of grief or walking the road of joy; but regardless of what road it was, we'd walk it together.

The clinic was going to call Brenda, not me, since she was the one who had the blood test done. I had to work that day, but both Dan and I wanted to hear the results together, so we waited until after I got off work to go over to the Vriezemas' together.

We walked in the door of Brenda's house and her first words were, "Don't know yet."

Brenda called the office a few times, but no one answered. We were a bit impatient. Finally around 2:45, the fertility clinic called. I just closed my eyes and held Dan's hand. I peeked and caught a glimpse of Brenda with a huge smile on her face as she gave the thumbs up.

BRENDA WAS PREGNANT.

The day prior, Brenda actually told me she thought she was. I had put my hand on her stomach and for some reason, I just knew. We both knew.

After Brenda hung up, we were all off the couch, and I'm not sure our feet landed before we hugged. We laughed. And laughed. I guess that is what you do when you are overflowing with excitement and releasing nerves, right? We felt like little kids who just found out they were going to Disney World! Not that we didn't believe God could do it or would do it, but to hear the word "pregnant," we were just amazed that God would choose us to experience that moment.

After we caught our breath from jumping and laughing, we sat and prayed. How do you even begin to put into words what we just heard? Thankfully, God could understand, even though I'm pretty sure our sentences didn't make any sense to the human ear. We were 11 months into the process and there we sat with Brenda pregnant with OUR babies. All we could do was give thanks to God! Our years and years of prayers had finally been answered!

(BRENDA)

I was pregnant with twins! Now I was completely sure that God was going to do this as every door was being opened wide. In my mind, the difficult part was behind us. I wasn't worried about the pregnancy one bit, since I was convinced that this was God's plan for Dan and Kristin. We were all on cloud nine.

Two days passed. Dan and I happened to be at Lowe's when we got a call from Brenda about whether her numbers were going up or not. If the numbers were going up, that meant the babies were growing. If not, well, we didn't want to go there. Dan answered and all I heard was the word awesome and then the numbers 123. At that point, I did the good ole golfer's cheer (you know the typical knee swing up and pump of the fist cheer).

It was crucial that Brenda's numbers at least doubled, so with her first blood test number being 49 and her second 123, that meant her hormones were increasing, and it was a healthy pregnancy. So on September 18 (Dan's birthday), we would have our first ultrasound. Dan of course said there couldn't be a better birthday present than to see our two babies for the first time!

We sped (or not sped, eh hem) to the Vriezemas' to celebrate. I skipped up to the door and was welcomed with a big hug from Brenda, as we just laughed again, with excitement, relief, and joy.

Yet there we sat. Dan unemployed, Brenda pregnant with our babies, and still so confused. The elders and pastor wrote a letter to the congregation explaining why Dan was "released." After reading the letter ourselves, we realized that it was rather vague, with misinterpretations and assumptions looming as to why he was let go. From what the letter said, we ourselves weren't even sure we knew why Dan was let go.

Dan asked the elders to make the reasons more clear to the church, but he was told that the letter had already been written, and for confidentiality reasons, they were going to leave it as is.

Sure enough, the misinterpretations and assumptions came. People were thinking Dan either harmed a youth group kid or had an affair. Now that left Dan and I having to defend our marriage, when his firing had absolutely *nothing* to do with that.

During all of the excitement around the twins, we were now trying to navigate our way through the uncertainty of unemployment and the confusion surrounding it. Our desire was to stay as close to Brenda as we could, so the farthest we wanted to move was about 1 ½ hours away, though we knew we had to go where God called. We had no idea where to even begin looking for jobs, but we knew God knew that He had a perfect place for us.

This just was not at all what we pictured this looking like.

CHAPTER 14

You Give And Take Away

Throughout the whole process, we knew one thing was certain: no matter what happened, God would allow what He deemed to be perfect and part of His plan to happen. God had blessed us with twins and the gift of friendship with the Vriezemas where nothing could break that tie.

On Monday, September 17, 2012, about two weeks after finding out Brenda was pregnant, I received a call from her after I arrived home from work that evening. I heard a shaky voice on the other end, as she began to tell me that she was bleeding a bit more than usual. Brenda had been spotting from the very beginning, and she repeatedly told me she didn't want to make me nervous or doubt, but she felt she needed to tell me.

I appreciated her letting me know, but my heart sank. It was a short conversation as we both really had nothing more to say.

After I hung up, I felt this void.

There was no easy way to tell Dan what Brenda had just called about. My heart was telling me it was more than just spotting, and that our two little babies were in the arms of our Heavenly Father that night; though everything in me tried to push those feelings aside.

We just couldn't even think about the possibility of a miscarriage and having to say goodbye to our two little babies. We had prayed for them for so long. There was no way this whole gestational carrier process would end in a miscarriage.

SEPTEMBER 18, 2012

The drive with Tim and Brenda to the fertility clinic that day wasn't what we all dreamed it would be. Though no one voiced it, Tim, Brenda, Dan, and I knew that just maybe it was the day that began a journey we prayed would never happen. The thought of the process not working was always a possibility, but we all were just so sure "this" was what God wanted for our lives, and that He would see it through to completion. A completion that in our minds meant Brenda giving birth two our two babies and us holding them in our arms.

As we headed back to the ultrasound room, my whole body started to shake. Dan and I held hands as the doctor slowly moved the probe over Brenda's abdomen. Initially not seeing anything on the monitor, in a soft voice he said, "Well, let's look over here, well, I don't see anything there, let me take a look over here…"

There were no babies to be found. No life anywhere. No heartbeats. No sight of anything.

An empty womb. Our deepest fears came true. God had taken our babies to their eternal home and we would never get a chance to hold them. Not any of us.

As the doctor finished the ultrasound, Dan and I stepped out of the room so Tim and Brenda could have a moment together. I just fell into Dan's arms. How do you even begin to comprehend that news after hearing the two babies you were planning and praying for, for the past 11 months, were no longer with us here on earth?

Tears fell from everyone as we made the especially long 1 ½ hour drive home. Did we hear correctly? Was there a chance the doctor made a mistake? Did God really take them home?

In the most tangible way possible, God saw our tears and reached out with His loving arms through the lyrics of the song, "Blessed Be Your Name," by Matt Redman:

"On the road marked with suffering, though there's pain in the offering, still, blessed be Your name. You give and take away, you give and take away..."

As we all soaked in the words, the tears turned to weeping. How could we say, "Blessed be your name," after losing and saying goodbye to our babies? After only three weeks old in the womb? They were an answer to years and years of prayer, and now God chose to take them away.

Brenda had one more appointment to double check her numbers to ensure that she indeed was no longer pregnant. It was in the 600 range, when the day before, it was at 1396. With the number being 600, there was some fear that the babies were stuck in her fallopian tubes, which would've put Brenda's life and the babies' lives at risk; thankfully that wasn't the case.

So instead of starting the journey of pregnancy together, we started the journey of grief together.

(BRENDA)

The four of us sat in the doctor's office looking at the monitor that showed my empty womb. The drive home from Grand Rapids was silent. There were no words. Actually, there was one word, "Why?"

Why would God lead us down this road for nothing?
Why did God "pull the rug out from under me?"
Why would He wait until now to slam the door shut?
Why didn't He close the door a long time ago, before there were actually two babies created?

Then it became...
Why is God so mean?
Why does God hate me so much?
Why would God use me to inflict so much pain and disappointment on Dan and Kristin?

In my pain and grief, I sunk into a deep dark place. There was so much loss surrounding this one event and I felt responsible. I must've heard God wrong. And as a result of this gestational carrier process, Dan lost his job as a youth pastor. They lost those two babies, their home, their friends, their youth group kids, and much, much more. They had such deep grief, yet they chose to cling to Jesus Christ for strength, comfort and peace. I, however, really struggled. How could I cling to the One who hurt me so deeply? How could I ever trust Him again?

Through the whole struggle of whether or not to create embryos to be adopted, we knew that God was calling us to give up everything for Him. We didn't know that it included our two little babies also. And now all I did was fear losing more.

When Dan lost his job, we lost the relationship we had with our youth group kids for reasons we did not understand. Dan had scheduled a bonfire before he was released, but we weren't allowed to go to it. It felt like we had committed a crime – what crime we didn't know, but it hurt deeply. Our youth group kids were incredibly confused, which didn't make the process of grieving any easier. We felt we couldn't talk to anyone, except our families and closest friends about our struggles, due to the separation agreement. But all of our grief was so intertwined, so in talking about the church issues, the babies would come up, and vice versa.

During such a difficult and trying time, we only felt shame from our very own church, and an arm that kept us at a distance.

After most embryo transfers, couples are given an ultrasound picture of the embryos all tucked away, safely in the womb. Unfortunately, the day of our transfer, the picture option on the ultrasound machine wasn't functioning. At the time I was a little disappointed, but little did I know that not having those pictures meant that one day we wouldn't have anything tangible to remember our two little babies by. The only "tangible" thing we had was the vision of an empty ultrasound screen.

It was tradition that every Thursday evening we'd go to my in-laws for supper. The Thursday night after initially finding out that Brenda was pregnant, we talked with our niece and nephews about their new cousins. Their biggest concern was what we would name them. At the time, one of our nephews, Levi, was into owls, so he suggested that we name our babies Hootie. We reminded him that there were two, so then he called them Hootie 1 and Hootie 2. Each time he brought up their names, we laughed, hoping those names wouldn't stick. In fact, when we showed him a picture of Dan, myself, and Brenda, he pointed at Brenda's stomach and said, "Hootie in there."

The Thursday after we lost the babies, Levi came up to Dan and excitedly said, "I have something for you." He handed Dan two paper owls he had made. Dan curiously asked him what they were for (not thinking anything of it) and he said, "Hootie."

When we were leaving that night, I asked Dan what the owls were for and he said, "I'll tell ya later." Then it hit me. We both looked at each other with tears streaming down our faces. We had such love for our babies already - the babies we'd never hold this side of Heaven.

Those two paper owls became the only tangible thing we had. They represented our dreams about who they would've looked like, how tall they would've been, and their gender. Everything. They brought many tears, yet so much joy. We decided to frame those two fragile, construction paper owls, and put them on our piano, next to our other family pictures, since they too were now part of our family. We wrote 9-17-12 in the corner, and to this day that picture still sits proudly on our piano with our other family pictures.

For a short time we are separated, but one day our family will be whole again.

Each person has their own "method" of grieving or way they think someone should grieve. Yet in reality, grief looks different for everyone.

One of the deepest struggles for us was that the gestational carrier process was over. For 11 months we were given so much hope. Our lives revolved around appointments, conversations, prayers, and the desire to just keep seeking after God's will in the process. God kept opening doors until finally He slammed the door shut. All our hopes and dreams of being parents one day were suddenly gone. We couldn't help but wonder what went wrong? What did WE do wrong?

We all believed the process was God's will and no one could take that from us or tell us it wasn't. But why did God choose, at just three weeks, to take them home?

I couldn't help but echo Brenda's desire: "I would love just a few minutes in God's physical presence so I can sort some things out with Him." Don't we all feel a sense of just wanting a few minutes with God sometimes? A few minutes of God's physical presence?

After Dan returned from a walk one day, he walked into the house and confidently said, "Kristin, we aren't supposed to worry because God will give us everything we need for the day." Part of me wanted to say, "Easy for you to say," but he knew exactly what he was saying. We were in this together. And God would not leave us in our grief.

Every day we'd spend time reading the sympathy cards we received in the mail from friends and family. I always wondered if sending a sympathy card was worth it, but even through a simple card, I often found incredible encouragement that spoke the very words I needed for that day; sometimes even in that moment.

Inside one specific card, the verse from 2 Corinthians 4:16-18 was written: "Therefore we do not lose heart. Though outwardly we are wasting away, yet inwardly we are being renewed day by day. For our light and momentary troubles are achieving for us an eternal glory that far outweighs them all. So we fix our eyes not on what is seen, but on what is unseen, since what is seen is temporary, but what is unseen is eternal."

We knew God was renewing us. We knew He was getting rid of the old so He could bring in the new. Yet we couldn't help but wonder, how much of the old was God going to get rid of? How much more chiseling had to occur? How much more pain and grief? Focusing on the unseen, proved to be the most difficult. We were focusing on those two babies, but God gently reminded us that our eyes are to always remain on Him.

The unseen.

CHAPTER 15

Putting Our Life in Boxes

A week after we lost our two babies, we started boxing up our house. When Dan lost his job, we knew we wouldn't be able to afford to live in our home. Not that we lived in a mansion, but we couldn't afford the mortgage on my part-time income, with an empty savings account, and bills still coming in. Dan's severance package could keep us afloat for a little while; but after that ended, we didn't want to be stuck wondering now what, and have to foreclose on our mortgage. The current housing market wasn't the greatest, and it would've been tough to sell our home for enough to pay off what we still owed on it. Fortunately, the rental market for a small house like ours was quite high. So before Dan's severance package ran out, we decided to get our house on the rental market.

At one point while packing up our belongings, we both sat on our basement stairs and wept. How much more?

We were supposed to be busy preparing a nursery, not emptying it out. While packing, I found little things that I was saving for our kids like books, and even my old sticker collection. I dreamed about sitting and reading those books to our babies. I dreamed about sharing my sticker collection with them. But now I just wanted to get rid of it all. Looking at those items only reminded me of what we'd just lost.

Dan, even in his brokenness, told me to hang onto all of it. Hang onto the hope that maybe one day, just ONE DAY, we would have children of our own. So in boxes they went.

Our parents were so gracious and willing to help in any way they could. Both offered their homes so we'd have a place to stay until God led us to our new destination. Since the past six years of our life were spent in Dan's hometown, we decided to live with Dan's parents. That way I could continue to work at my part-time job as well.

When we officially moved out one cold and rainy Saturday, I remember being completely exhausted in every way possible. We walked downstairs into the basement of Dan's parent's house to get our new room set up, and saw that our bed was all put together. I just cried. To have something of comfort that we still had, something as simple as a bed to lay our heads on, all set up with the lamp on the nightstand lit, was such a gift.

Maybe this grief journey was possible.

As much as we felt the sting of grief, Tim and Brenda did all the more. Not only were they grieving emotionally, but Brenda's body now to had to finish the process of miscarrying. To this day, I still have a hard time thinking about it without tears. My dear friend, the woman who chose to give up the comforts of her own life so we could have children, would now go through even more pain, all so that we had the chance at newborn life. How could I ever thank her enough? How could I ever repay her?

From the very beginning, we knew our friendship was indescribable. It went far beyond any worldly standard. It was something that never wavered, even through the deepest of griefs. Before we even started the process, our church had cautioned us for fear of what it might do to our relationship with them if the process was unsuccessful. We appreciated their concern, but politely set it aside because we knew our friendship was much deeper than any circumstance. Even though the unimaginable happened, our friendship stood. We all dealt with the pain in our own ways, all needing time to grieve, but we still cried together, prayed together, laughed together, and got through it, together.

(BRENDA)

Thankfully, God had blessed me with a husband with faith, patience, and deep love for me. He listened to me, he prayed over me, and he always pointed me back to God; to the One I believed hurt me. He kept reminding me that we walked where we thought the Spirit was leading. Deep down I knew Tim was right, and that God was the only One who could heal me of my pain and lift me from my dark place. And so I began to cry out to God to heal my brokenness, and to remove my pain and guilt. And God, in His lavish grace, did. Little by little, the wounds were healing. He spoke tenderly to me through His Word and songs, convincing me of His love for me. It's as if He has taken my face in His hands and spoke His love into my soul. Things I have known in my head about God's grace, I now know in my heart. He has a plan and a purpose for me, and that plan is good. Because of this event in our lives, we are eyewitnesses to the power of God and recipients of

His grace. He never left me alone. Funny thing is, I don't need all of my "why" questions answered anymore. I am able to see how God has used this experience to shape me, to draw me to Himself, how He has used this for my good, for Dan and Kristin's good, and for His glory.

A friend had sent Dan a devotional she had read by Chuck Swindoll called, "The Impossible Is God's Ideal" that put into words what we could not:

I'd like to underline a major truth in this world of ours that I don't pretend to understand. Here it is: The best framework for the Lord God to do His most ideal work is when things are absolutely impossible and we feel totally unqualified to handle it.

That's His favorite circumstance. Those are His ideal working conditions.

God does His most magnificent work when the situation seems totally impossible from a human point of view, and we feel absolutely unprepared and unable to do anything about it, yet our eyes are on Him… That's when God rolls up His big sleeves and says, "Step back out of the way a moment, and watch Me work."

Time after time, He brings us to our absolute end and then proves Himself faithful.[10]

Those words brought freedom, a calmness of heart, and relief. Like I said, we often felt we had to have the "right" answer to silence the critics, even in our grief. We felt completely unqualified to handle what felt like the impossible. Unqualified to do the gestational carrier process. Unqualified to do embryo donation. Unqualified to handle grief. I felt like those words finally gave me the freedom to step out of the way and watch God work because He is the one who qualifies and does the impossible.

Even though we sometimes felt we'd never find relief from our grief, we hung onto our belief that God would prove Himself faithful.

And He did.

While grieving the loss of those two little babies, we were encouraged to get away for a while, where we had time to think and breathe. Time away from the hurts of what was now becoming a chapter of our past.

It's not that we didn't have the time; we just didn't have the money. Then one day, out of the blue, came a knock on our door. It was a friend of ours standing there with a coffee can in hand, full of money. She encouraged us to use it for that very purpose. That only solidified the answer to our prayers of whether or not we should go.

When we thought about a place of retreat, refreshment, and peace, we kept coming back to the lake where my parents rented a cottage every summer. It was that place of peace, relaxation, and of good memories. It felt like a home away from home.

We knew the request was a bit odd since it was the off season, but we got the gumption to ask the people we rented from if they still had their cottage open in October. We had a set price in our heads and knew if it was above that price, we weren't meant to go.

Little did we know that God had this all planned out. After a recent trip overseas, the family had been wondering how God could use them specifically in other's lives, such as offering a place of peace and rest. Needless to say, God joined our stories together to create

114

this beautiful answer to both of our prayers. A place we could stay for free. I was brought to tears of joy and humbleness, for how God knit together both of our prayers, for such a time as that.

Our first night there, the northern lights glowed as we heard the owls hooting in the distance. It was God's gentle wink to us that He was present and didn't forget about those two Hooties in Heaven.

One thing Dan couldn't wait to do as a father was take his kids fishing. When we left for our getaway, he said that even though he'd never be able to take them fishing, he still wanted to take them in a different way. So he put the picture frame with our two paper owls from our nephew in a plastic baggie, and took them fishing for the first and last time. A memory worth making and a dream worth living.

Also while on the getaway, we quickly learned how much those two little babies had already become such a big part of our lives, even though they were only three gestational weeks old. Dan saw a little hat that read "My First Fishing Hat" in a local store. I had to walk away because otherwise I was going to be a complete basket case in the middle of the store; but it was one of those items that every dad probably gets their firstborn as a memory and keepsake. Let's be honest - the kid probably couldn't care less, but to the parent, that memento meant the world. Dan had to leave that hat behind.

It was those little things, those little reminders to us, of just how deeply we loved those babies and how deeply we missed them already. We never knew a love could be so deep for two children we had never even met.

That week, many tears were shed and much healing occurred. We reflected, read about grief, talked about grief, and dealt with grief, together. We even were able to laugh a little too - especially since Dan was beating me in every game of Skip-Bo we played. I should note, thanks to that trip, we now having a running score (best out of three) of Skip-Bo to this day.

It was difficult to understand the whys. In the midst of our grief, I kept feeling this nudge from God to let go. I even felt that nudge before the babies were created, but I didn't know what that meant. I didn't know at that time it meant our babies, our home, our youth group kids, and our church, but God can give and take away as He pleases because everything is a gift. We weren't entitled to, nor did we deserve anything of what we had.

We really felt God telling us, "Sterks, your life is NOT your own, so live for Me and Me alone!" Was I really willing to give up anything and everything if God asked me to? Even our very own children? There were no logical answers, but that was where we had to allow our faith to step in.

Deuteronomy 29:29 says: "The secret things belong to the Lord our God, but the things revealed belong to us and to our children forever, that we may follow all the words of this law."

Some live their lives trying to find a logical or practical answer to everything. What, then, is the point of faith? When answers were hard to find and understanding far off in the distance, Proverbs 3:5-6 came to mind: "Trust in the Lord with all your heart and lean not on your own understanding; in all your ways submit to him, and he will make your paths straight." What peace those verses gave during a time that seemed so uncertain.

In times of difficulty, it is hard to ignore the story of Job; the man who lost his family and everything he owned. Job eventually threw up his hands in Job 7:19-20 and said, "Will you never look away from me, or let me alone even for an instant? If I have sinned, what have I done to you, you who see everything we do? Why have you made me your target? Have I become a burden to you?"

Job probably felt like a target and at times, we did too. Why our babies? Why both of them? Why the job? Why our home? Why our youth group kids?

It was all so that God's name would be glorified. In the midst of all of those questions, the real question was Who would we represent despite the circumstances? Were we representing Christ's sovereignty in our life the best way we could so that God's work could be displayed?

My basketball coach from my junior year of high school often said before we stepped out on the court: "Remember who you are representing." No matter what happened, trials and triumphs included, who was getting the glory, and who were we representing through our responses to those who questioned our every move?

All we wanted was for God to get the glory.

Seeing what God was doing in our life also increased our love for those who had experienced loss. I once heard it said that grief opens the door for more compassion. To this day, I have a hard time not tearing up over hearing of loss. Partially I think it brings me back to our time of grief, but ultimately it is a realization that our world is broken and painful. It makes me want to reach out a hand of love, knowing the journey can be incredibly heartbreaking.

Our friends and family understood and allowed us to grieve in our own way. Many shared their stories of loss: loss of children (born and unborn), loss of spouses, and loss of friends. All stories that reached deep into our hearts and encouraged us to keep going, all for the glory of God.

Again, back to Job (like I said, you can't talk about grief without talking about Job).

Even though Job felt like a target, he continued to praise God, even though he thought he'd never again see happiness (Job 7:7). Job 1:21 says, "Naked I came from my mother's womb and naked I will depart. The Lord gave and the Lord has taken away; may the name of the Lord be praised."

A week after our babies left their temporary home here on earth, I desperately wondered how I was supposed to PRAISE God? How could there be any joy in loss? How could thankfulness pour from my heart after saying goodbye? Then Dan reminded me of the same song that we listened to on the way home from that grief-filled day on September 18, 2012: "Blessed Be Your Name." A song not sung without tears flowing, but a song that taught us to let go, let God, and give it all to Him.

I had to learn what it meant to find joy and hope in God again, which brought me to a whole new understanding of His unconditional love. When I felt I had nothing left to give, it was God who continued to put His arms underneath mine, lifted me back to my feet, dusted me off, and told me to keep going. Even when He gives and takes away, He truly is a good, good God, worthy of our praise.

Dealing with grief is a choice. Every day I had to make the choice to not stay angry or frustrated, but to have the faith that God had a greater plan. There were times when I wanted to go back to our life before we lost our babies. Yet I had to let this mold us into the beings God was working to form. It was a choice to not let fear and worry drive me. It was a choice to keep following God and His will for my life.

Choose to not be silent in your grief, no matter what level that grief may be. I used to fear people's responses when I told them I was unable to have my own children. I felt this sense of shame, that something was wrong with me. After I made the decision to be open about our inability to have children, it opened the door for some very intimate conversations with others who also struggled to have children. And now I was having those intimate conversations with those who had lost children.

Don't let shame or fear keep you silent because those two things are not of God's character. Find that trusted friend to confide in and walk the road with.

And I say with complete confidence, it was worth the choice to be vulnerable and to keep following Christ.

CHAPTER 16

Moving Forward

Before God could call us back into youth ministry, He had a lot of healing to do in our lives. Not only were we back to square one with no kids, we were now grieving the loss of two little lives.

To me, a perfect day would consist of drinking hot cocoa while blogging, crocheting an afghan, or making cards. Now that our life came to a halt, and I actually had the time to do those things, it was the last thing I wanted to do. I didn't want to rest; I wanted our babies back. I wanted our life to feel normal again.

I used to think that moving forward meant I had to be okay with our past and with or losses. I was afraid to move on because I feared forgetting about our babies. I feared losing the memories. I felt that moving forward meant I had to be okay with them dying. I have since learned that moving forward means choosing to believe that God is in control and to believe in the good plan He has for our lives.

So I started to blog, make cards, crocheted a few afghans, and even drank some hot cocoa.

During this lull in our life, I was attending a small Bible study that Brenda had in her home. For years, she had a group of ladies over every Thursday morning to discuss a book, read Scripture, and to pray. At the time, we were studying, "Life Principles from the Old Testament" by Wayne Barber, and one particular lesson that stood out to me was about Noah.

The story of Noah is one of those Sunday school stories that you learn as a wee little one. God tells Noah to build an ark after the people repeatedly and unrepentantly disobeyed God. So, with the laughter of many watching him, Noah built this ark in the middle of a desert. Today if someone built an ark in the middle of the Arizona desert because they thought a flood was coming, we would think they were crazy! Well, sure enough, God sent rain for 40 days and 40 nights. Enough rain that it covered every last corner of the earth; just imagine that.

Even though God saved Noah and his family from the flood that destroyed the entire earth, Noah still had to experience many trials. Noah built an ark when everyone else and their brother thought he was crazy. He still had to go through the flood. He still had to watch the world get destroyed. Noah still had to go through much trouble and hardship to see the rainbow on the other side. This quote really caught my attention:

"Quite often we look to God for deliverance from trouble, yet that is not always His way. Sometimes God determines that He can get greater

glory by safely bringing us through trouble rather than avoiding it...God took him through the flood. God does not always deliver us from trouble; sometimes He delivers us in the midst of it. God's deliverance for Noah didn't mean that he had no troubles, but that he had God's provision in the midst of his troubles."[11]

After reading that, I found it difficult to think that God was getting greater glory through our pain, instead of our babies being born, but He had a purpose in everything He allowed. God is in the business of creating a new self in each of those who are in Him. God brought Noah into a whole new world on the other side of his trial and maybe that was His plan for us too. We just wanted to cling to God with that same trust that He would do the same for us.

There was an older couple from our former church named Joe and Karen, and together, they had a passion for missions. After Dan lost his job in September, he would often go on walks through town just to be alone and think. One day while on one of those walks, Dan ran into Joe, and he mentioned to Dan that he was planning a mission trip down to Belize in early January. If Dan was available they would love for him to come along. Not knowing where we'd be or what we'd be doing in four months, Dan told Joe that he would think about it.

Well, after four months of not thinking about it, Dan saw a post on Facebook from Joe about the mission trip he was planning in a few weeks, and how they were going to fix the roof at a medical clinic. So far the team consisted of just Joe and Karen, and they needed help with the physical labor. Later that night Dan mentioned to me that Joe was looking for help and wondered if there was any way he could go along. Money was tight, and we weren't sure how we would pay for a trip like that, but I felt it would be so good for Dan to get out, serve others, and feel useful again. So I told Dan to call Joe and express his interest; we'd figure out how to pay for it later.

While Dan was over at Joe and Karen's working on the logistics of the trip, Joe shared with him that an anonymous donor had offered to cover the entire cost of the trip for Dan. We didn't have a clue who this person was, but we were so grateful for their generosity.

As soon as Dan walked in the door, he couldn't wait to tell me the news. Somebody had offered to cover the entire cost! What a blessing! While Dan was mid-sentence telling me this great news, his phone rang. It was Joe calling to tell us that this anonymous donor was offering to cover the cost of the trip if I wanted to go as well. I broke down in tears, feeling so undeserving that someone would bless us with this gift. An expensive one at that!

To this day, we still do not know who paid both of our ways, but talk about God's sustaining grace!

So in the middle of January, we left for Belize. It was a short five-day trip, but nonetheless, a trip packed with opportunities to minister to the Belizeans. We knew a roof had to be repaired and that we were going to be ministering to the homeless, but we had no idea what God had in store for us.

That trip proved to be a turning point in both of our lives. It was on that trip that we felt God calling us to continue a life in youth ministry. It was in Belize that God set up divine appointments to show us that He was still in control, despite how out of control we felt.

While there, every day one of our team members encouraged us with this: "When you follow God, He will make clear what He wants you to do in a given day." Well, I call that a breeding ground for divine appointments.

One day we went into a Belizean neighborhood that was built over a swampy marsh that also served as the city dump. In some parts of the neighborhood, there were no streets, just rocks that served as stepping stones from house to house. All of the single-room homes (more like huts) were built out of scrap wood and rusty sheet metal that sat on stilts over the water. The bathrooms in these homes consisted of an open hole in the floor, with direct access to the swampy water below. It was also next to a large cemetery called the Burial Grounds. Because of the marshy landscape, people were buried above ground, with brick being used as a coffin. The stench wasn't for the weak stomach. The moisture from the burial grounds was something that never dissipated because of the marsh.

The week prior to our being in that neighborhood, unbeknownst to us, there were murders, execution style. As a result, the U.S. had deemed it unsafe to go to Belize. It was also clear that some of the children there were taught to not like the white American. Sitting in the back of our rented pickup truck, as we drove by, children would make their hands into the shape of a gun and pretend to shoot us.

Despite the uncertainty, we tried to live out the motto we repeated often that week: "Go all out, no fear." We knew God had us there for a reason and whatever happened, we prayed His will would be done. In fact, most of the people we encountered and spoke with, were very open and hungry for God's Word. Which, speaking of hunger, we took the opportunity to share about God's love if the opportunity presented itself, but we first gave out beans and rice to meet their physical needs. That simple act of handing out food to a hungry community quickly opened doors.

One particular path we took to get to a hut consisted of jumping over puddles and tiptoeing on what was left of a broken walkway made of stone, tin, and wood pieced together. A grandma was seated outside, holding a beautiful baby girl. Language was sometimes a barrier, but no words were needed with her smile. The grandma gave me the baby, which blessed my empty arms incredibly. Seconds later, a young woman about 25, named Natasha (who was the baby's mom), came out as we were handing out beans and rice. You could see the plea on the grandma's face that food was hard to come by in their home.

After exchanging words for a few minutes, we walked away feeling this supernatural bond with Natasha. She seemed lost in life, looking for something. What that something was we weren't sure, but Dan and I felt this tug for this aching mama.

It was clear from her tears and clothing that she was seeking love in all the wrong places. She was a woman who seemed broken on the inside, but was as beautiful and put together as you could be on the outside. As we said our goodbyes and made our way back down the broken boardwalk, we heard a faint voice. Just before we started back down the gravel road toward the rest of the group, we glanced back and saw Natasha tiptoeing down the pathway.

With more tears in her eyes, she asked if she could have more beans and rice. At that moment, that divine appointment, it was clear she needed to be told about the love of Christ. Dan and I both shared with her how much she was loved. Loved by a God who would never abandon her, who would never let her go, but had come to save her.

We asked if we could pray with her and she quickly said yes. As we bowed our heads, I looked up and saw tears just streaming down her face. After Dan finished praying, I told her I'd continue to pray for her, and one day, would see her in Heaven. It only took three minutes for us to form a bond with Natasha and it only took three minutes for her to realize she was loved by God.

I gave her a hug (a hug she clearly longed for), as she begged us to not leave. I felt the same; I felt I was leaving part of my heart with her.

After that encounter, everything changed for me. I stepped back in the truck and just wept. The hurt and pain Natasha felt, the love she desired so deeply, the needs she had, the little baby, everything, reached down into the deepest parts of my heart. I wanted to just grab her and take her back with me to the United States. Not that I was her savior, but I wanted to share more about THE Savior. It was a very surreal moment for both Dan and me. Here we were, viewed as the rich Americans who had everything, and there stood Natasha living in such poverty. Yet in her arms, she held the one thing that we so desperately wanted. A baby of our own.

God used that divine appointment to remind us that we could be used by God. That He had a purpose and that, yes, we could hear God's voice. It was a voice that told us He wasn't done with us, even though we felt others were.

It was then that we felt the call to stay in youth ministry. Up until that point, we weren't sure that was even what we were meant to do. When Dan was let go from our previous church, the letter that was sent to the congregation by the church leadership stated that they had serious concerns about Dan's Biblical discernment and, as a result, felt that Dan was no longer able to lead the youth of the church. Those words cut deep and started to cause doubt in Dan's mind. After this trip, we returned home saying, "Yes, God still wants to use us in ministry."

One night while in Belize, Dan was catching up on emails. He called me over to the kitchen table at the ministry house where we were staying, and said he received an email from the search committee at a church in Minnesota.

Let me back up a second. A month prior, Dan was in the interviewing process with another church, but saw an ad advertising a job opportunity in Prinsburg/Willmar, Minnesota. Minnesota seemed so far away from family and everything that was familiar to us, so he waited until the last possible week to send his résumé. Plus, it was a position that combined the youth from two different churches, which was something we hadn't done before, so we were uncertain how that would all work. We later learned that his application was technically late because the deadline for résumés in the ad was a misprint, and the church had stopped taking them two weeks prior. Talk about a great start in the process.

Now back to Dan sitting at that kitchen table in Belize. He opened the email and the search committee desired to set up a phone interview as soon as we got back from our trip. Dan had the phone interview, and the following day he received a call from the head of the search committee asking if we'd be willing to come out for a face-to-face interview. That same day Dan also heard from the other church he was interviewing at, that he didn't get the position. The door was suddenly flung wide open for the possibility of moving to Minnesota.

About a week after the initial phone interview, we rented a vehicle and drove out to Minnesota. We never imagined living in Minnesota, but hey, why not see what happened with the interview? It wasn't like we had anything else going on!

The drive out to Minnesota was absolutely beautiful - if you enjoy a country drive that is. You have to make your way through Chicago first if coming from Michigan, but from that point on, it is an open landscape. The rolling hills of Wisconsin were frosted with a fresh coat of snow and the trees were sporting their white winter coats. We arrived in Willmar, which is about two hours directly west of Minneapolis, settled into our hotel room, and tried to find a place to eat. Most restaurant names were unfamiliar, so when we saw good ole Perkins down the road, we knew that was our answer.

Our first encounter with someone from Minnesota outside of the hotel receptionist, was our waitress. I've never met someone (to this day) who had such a thick Minnesotan accent as she did! Welcome to Minnesoooota, eh? We both looked at each other and said, "They really do talk like that!"

The next morning Dan had breakfast with Steve, one of the pastors, and came back from that meeting confirming that this was the place we were meant to be. Dan shared our story with him and he accepted it with open arms and love. At one point, Dan shared with Steve that right now, more than anything else, he just wanted our two babies back. Steve looked at Dan, and with tears in his eyes said, "I have seven kids right now, but 18 years ago my wife and I lost our first son when she was eight months pregnant. There isn't a day that has gone by that I haven't longed to have that one back."

We knew wherever we ended up next that our story came with us. So it was comforting to Dan to know that Steve related to the loss we experienced. When Dan was telling me about their meeting, he looked at me and said, "I need to work with this guy."

We went to lunch with two of the search committee members, took a tour of the town, and then had the formal interview. I should say "formal" loosely because talk about a laid-back interview. It felt as if we had known them all for years. After the interview there was a meal provided and a meet and greet with the congregations and youth group kids. It didn't take long for us to feel like we had known everyone for years. The jokes and laughter made us feel right at home.

At the meet and greet, Dan also met Jeff, one of the other pastors. Jeff is a say-it-how-it-is guy, and out of nowhere he asked Dan, "So what happened at your past church? Why did you leave?" Instantly Dan shrunk back in fear. Did he really want to get into all of that right now? Cautiously, Dan began to explain what had happened in our previous church five months prior. When Dan finished talking, Jeff looked at Dan and said, "You know the last two churches I worked at ended in an ugly separation as well." Instantly Dan knew he had to work with this pastor as well. The two pastors that Dan would be working with had both shared the same emotions and hurts that Dan was feeling at that very moment.

At the end of the night we were told that the search committee was going to recommend Dan to the council. As we laid our heads down that night, we knew the next time we'd come to Minnesota was to start a new chapter of our life there.

And that is exactly what happened. Dan was offered the position, he accepted, and two weeks later we went back out to Minnesota to find housing. With each drive out there, we knew it would be bittersweet to say goodbye to family, but we knew it was where God wanted us.

CHAPTER 17

This Is Where the Healing Begins

On Thursday, March 7, we hauled all of our belongings to Prinsburg, Minnesota. It was a bitter cold day with plenty of snow on the ground, but the clear roads made a perfect pathway for us. There was an army of youth group kids and people from the churches, waiting at our new house, to help us unpack our moving truck. One of our soon-to-be best friends, Trapper, pulled out our snow blower and yelled, "Hey, what's this for?" Thinking it was a trick question, Dan sheepishly said, "To clear the driveway?" To which Trapper replied, "Well, you're going to need a bigger one!" What a welcome to Minnesota! There is a reason people affectionately call it "Minne-snow-ta."

The move went smoothly, and we found ourselves starting over, which was exactly what we needed. Everything was new. The people, the area, the stores, the climate, the scenery, everything.

We quickly learned that God brought us to Minnesota for more than just a job. At the time, we didn't realize how much healing still had to occur until the wounds were opened up again. God knew we needed our pastors and new friends so that we could work through some of our past hurts. Healing was something only God could bring, but He knew to accomplish His purposes, we had to move to Minnesota.

We had been living in Minnesota for about two months when the due date of our babies came. Ironically that date fell very close to Mother's Day, which didn't necessarily make it any easier.

Though it was a difficult week, we knew God had a grander purpose through all our wonderings about the whys and the timing of it all. In fact, I wrote a blog post about those very wonders; but with each one, God trumped it with His grace.

We wondered why so soon? God reminded us time is not in our hands.
We wondered why both? God reminded us He is the Author of life.
We wondered why not just a glimpse of an ultrasound? God reminded us faith is unseen.
We wondered why only three weeks in the womb? God reminded us that He gave us the gift of parenthood.
We wondered why such pain? God reminded us that He is the God of all comfort.
We wondered why so many tears? God reminded us that He works for the good of those who love Him and are called according to His purposes (Romans 8).

We wondered why my heart condition? God reminded us that our bodies are not our own, but we belong both body and soul, to our faithful Savior, Jesus Christ.

We wondered why the days of utter grief? God reminded us that He walked this path first and we do not walk it alone.

We wondered what life with our two babies here on this earth would look like? God reminded us in Proverbs 16:9, "In their hearts humans plan their course, but the Lord establishes their steps."

For years we prayed that one day God would perform a miracle and heal my heart, but we had to come to grips with the circumstances we were in. If God didn't heal me, it didn't mean He didn't hear or love me any less. He still loved me the same, even though we were left with empty arms.

When Dan and I left West Michigan to move out to Minnesota, we left with a feeling of despair and lost hope of ever having our own child someday. Dan left with a lot of anger and confusion with the leadership at our previous church, and the way he chose to deal with those emotions, was to suppress and not deal with them. After all, it is easier to tuck emotions away than to actually let them out and talk about the war raging inside the mind and heart. Well, that raging war began to slowly change who Dan was.

For Dan, he didn't want to talk about kids. He didn't want to be around little kids and didn't even want to hold my little niece in the hospital on the day she was born. If he secluded himself from anything that would remind him of the babies we didn't have, then he didn't have to walk down the road of losing hope of one day having our own. He rationalized that it was easier to not have hope at all, than to have hope and face the disappointment when everything fell apart.

While Dan was suppressing the hope of one day having our children to hold in our arms, he was also suppressing the anger over the ugly separation from our previous church. Typically, Dan is a very patient man who deals with other people with a lot of grace. That all started to erode as he suppressed that anger. The patience and grace he once had was slowly being replaced by a short fuse and a bitter heart. While out in public, he hid the war raging inside; but at home, I often bore the brunt of the emotional war that was going on inside his heart and mind. While driving home one evening together, every emotion he had refused to take care of, exploded with four words I said to Dan.

He doesn't mind me sharing this tidbit, since it was a game changer for the both of us. That evening while driving home, he felt pressure building in his bowels. Thinking he could get away with relieving a little pressure, ever so slyly he let some gas escape. He quickly realized he wasn't going to get away with it, so trying to be funny, he rolled my window down a little so that the wonderful new aroma would waft over my way, and out of the car. I looked over at him and said, "You are so stupid."

Instantly those words cut into him and brought out every suppressed emotion. He slammed on the brakes and pulled over to the side of the road and yelled, "Don't you ever say that to me again!"

He was so angry, and later on he confessed that in the moment, he contemplated kicking me out of the car and making me walk home. Thankfully his irrational thinking left quickly, and he decided against it. Needless to say, it was a very quiet drive the rest of the way home. That quiet drive gave him time to think about what had just happened. Here I was left in the passenger seat wondering the same thing! That ugly separation from our previous church and being told he was basically worthless as a youth pastor, caused him to burrow those emotions deep inside and he had yet to deal with them.

That night after we got home, he realized that to deal with his anger, he had to forgive those who had hurt him. At the time though, he didn't feel that he could honestly do that.

About a month after verbally vomiting all over me, Dan traveled to New York City for a mission trip with a group of kids from the local Christian High School. One afternoon while he was lying on his bed reading, Bryan, one of the other adult leaders and one of the fiercest prayer warriors we've ever met, gently sat down on the edge of Dan's bed. In a very cautious voice he said, "Dan, I need to tell you that during my prayers recently, I have had an image of hope for both you and Kristin. Hope that you'd be able to have kids of your own."

Instantly Dan's brain was flooded with a rush of emotions. How could Bryan sit there and tell him he had an image of hope for us? We had been praying for years that God would heal my heart so that we could have our own children, and still my heart wasn't healthy. We had literally put all our eggs in one basket in attempting to have our own kids through Brenda, and losing much in the process, including Dan's job. We had recently concluded that maybe God didn't have kids in mind for us, and we had finally become content with that.

In Dan's mind, at that time, he was thinking there was no way he was going down that road again of getting his hopes up that we could have our own children, only to have them dashed away again. He didn't know what to say to Bryan, so all he could work out was "Bryan, I am afraid."

To top it all off, Bryan added, "But I also see that there is some forgiveness that needs to happen in your heart first." Again, his brain was flooded with emotions, only this time instead of fear, it was anger seeping into his thoughts. He was tired of people telling him that he had to forgive the pastor and elders at our previous church. Dan knew in his head he needed to forgive them, but in his heart, he just couldn't do it. He just couldn't seem to let go of the hurt.

Again, he didn't know what to say, but was able to mumble something along the lines of, "Wow Bryan, that's a tough one." Then in typical Bryan fashion, he asked if he could pray for Dan right then and there. Bryan grabbed the two other men they were sharing a room with and the three of them prayed over Dan that God would restore hope for Dan and me, and that He would also soften Dan's heart so that he could forgive.

The rest of the afternoon Dan lay in his bed, thinking about forgiveness. He didn't even want to approach the hope thing yet. While he was laying there, he kept holding onto the thought that if he forgave the pastor and elders at our previous church, then it meant that they won, or somehow got away with it. After laying there for over an hour, he finally realized that in holding onto his anger and not forgiving them, he was letting them win every day because it was controlling him and turning him into someone he didn't want to be. He *had* to let go of his anger and forgive them. At that moment he began praying, telling God he forgave the pastor and elders at our previous church, and that he wasn't going to hold onto his anger anymore.

That night, since it was the week of Easter Sunday, Dan and the mission group went to the Brooklyn Tabernacle for their presentation of the Passion of the Christ. If you've never been to the Brooklyn Tabernacle, it is a place you need to experience for yourself, so I was told by Dan. The place is enormous, with a seating capacity of 3,200 people in their sanctuary alone. It is your classic old vaudeville theater from the early 1900's with high vaulted ceilings, like something you would see in the Capitol building, with a giant chandelier hanging in the center. Just to walk into the place is apparently breath-taking.

Dan said as the lights went down and the music started to play while the narrator spoke, his mind drifted off to the idea of hope; hope that one day we'd have a child of our own. Dan found himself asking, "Do I want to venture down that road again?" The images of holding a newborn baby, wiping a snotty nose, putting bandaids on scraped knees, teaching his little buddy how to fish, and joining forces to pick on me, all dreams Dan had once entertained, all came oozing back into his mind like blood from a fresh-picked scab. Slowly a tear began to well up in his eyes as more images he had learned to suppress, began to re-emerge in his head.

He didn't want anyone else to notice his puffy eyes that were swelled with held back tears, but then realized that they were at the part of the Passion of the Christ where Jesus was being flogged and beaten, and everyone else had puffy eyes too. Finally, he silently mouthed the words, "I want to be a dad again."

Instantly the flood gates opened, his eye lids gave way, and the tears just started to pour out. As the play finished and the lights came back on, he looked around and could tell everyone else had been fighting back tears as well. Everyone assumed that his tear-streaked face was because of the powerful emotion displayed in the Passion of the Christ. Little did they all know that hope had re-entered his life, and he wanted to be a daddy in the worst way.

A few weeks later, Dan and I attended a reunion party with people who went on the New York mission trip. I wasn't sure I wanted to go since I hadn't been on the trip, but many of our youth group kids would be there, and it'd be good to see them all again.

While the kids were eating pizza in the fellowship hall, Bryan asked me if Dan had told me about their conversation in New York about having hope. Of course Dan had told me about it, and in fact, Dan had called me that night while he was in New York. Bryan said, "Well we would love to pray over you some time if that is okay with you." I told Bryan that would be great, and that I had a heart appointment coming up in a few days. Well, there's no time like the present, so Bryan said, "Let's pray right now then!"

So Bryan, Pastor Steve, and our friend Perry, circled around us and prayed. Pastor Steve brought out some anointing oil, spread it on my forehead, which was a first for me, and prayed that at this time next year, we would be holding a baby of our own. When I heard those words, I wasn't sure what to think. For so many years we had been told no, and had lost hope. I knew God could make those dreams come true, but I fully admit, I had much doubt.

"Delight yourself in the Lord, and He will give you the desires of your heart." Psalm 37:4

I have always struggled with that verse. I believe that Scripture is true and without any error, but at the same time, in my human mind, I struggled to understand how this verse was true. I know, ye of little faith, but I had lost faith in that verse. The problem though was that I was reading it all wrong.

The first part of the verse is essential and fundamental. Without applying, living out, and submitting to the will of God, the second half is not a guarantee.

The night before my appointment, Dan stood in front of our youth group kids and talked about that very thing. He confessed that even though he desired his own child, maybe it wasn't God's plan; and he was okay with it. We wanted what God wanted. Dan was willing to give up that dream and delight himself in the Lord first, and the amount of peace that came out of him sharing that, gave us a pep in our step for the next day.

May 15, 2014 came around, and like clock-work, I had yet another yearly heart appointment.

For the past 13 years, I heard the same words, over and over again: *The mitral valve is getting worse and you will need surgery in the near future.*

Thirteen years of hearing that made me wonder if the day would ever come. In fact, I was (almost) to the point of just wanting to get the surgery done with. I was weary from hearing "near future" and just wished I could put the surgery behind me and move on. Not that open heart surgery is something that people request, but for me it was inevitable at some point.

This ordinary heart checkup in May happened to fall two days before our babies would've turned one, had they been born on their scheduled due date, which made the reality of our situation of not being able to have children even harder. Thinking about them celebrating their first birthday in Heaven made us long to celebrate with them, but we knew they would be having the best party.

The night before the appointment, as I was lying in bed praying and thinking about the events of the next day, I jokingly said to Dan, "What if the doctor told us I could get pregnant?" I chuckled after I said it, and Dan, well, I can't remember if he said anything, but it was a fleeting thought.

We didn't joke about that idea much. In fact, we rarely ever talked about it. Yes, we prayed for it, but that was about it. We both knew that was the one thing we still desired, but talking about it only made the pain of what we couldn't have, worse.

We drove two hours east to Minneapolis where my heart doctor was located. It was the first time we had been at this clinic because when we first moved to Minnesota the year prior, I was seen by a local specialist. After that specialist looked at my ECHO and previous heart history, he said he wasn't equipped or knowledgeable enough to deal with my situation. That's why we had to go all the way to Minneapolis to see a specialist. We appreciated his blunt and honest opinion, but I must admit those aren't the words a heart patient wants to hear.

Back to the appointment. The sequence of events was just like any other heart appointment - same tests, same questions, same everything. Nothing new.

As always, the medical imager and nurse commented about my heart history of ALCAPA. When the medical imager said, "You are one of the few, the proud..." I was reminded of just how rare it was to live with a condition such as that, for 17 years. Not only that, but the RN said I was "one in a million" because it wasn't every day they met a patient like me. By God's grace I was still alive.

As we waited to meet with the doctor, I was getting a bit impatient. I felt this quivering in my heart as nerves started to fill my body. I sat on my hands, trying to mask the shaking as I waited to hear the words: open heart surgery.

Our life was about to be drastically changed, but not by the three words "open heart surgery" that we were expecting.

As my doctor reviewed my test results, she said that my mitral valve was only mildly to moderately leaking. That came as a bit of a surprise since for years I was told my valve was moderately to severely leaking, being on the brink of needing surgery. She went on to explain that everything looked very good.

For those few seconds we wondered how a leaky faucet (my valve) was leaking less. Usually leaks only get worse, right?

Dan quickly looked at the doctor, then me, then back at her and asked, "What does this mean for pregnancy?"

Her next six words knocked us out of our seats.

"I SEE NO PROBLEM WITH IT."

Six words that seemed medically impossible. Words that we had longed to hear for eight years of our marriage. Words filled with so much hope. Words filled with so much grace. Words that God used to remind us that He was faithful and never done, even when we had lost all hope in having our own children.

We were speechless. Joy-filled tears ran down my cheeks as I muttered to the doctor, while trying to gain my composure, "We have been waiting eight years to hear this."

The look on her face was one of, "What just happened here?" She had no clue. She had just met us and all she did was report the test results. She had *no* clue we longed to have children. That, of course, wasn't in the notes. She just thought she was telling us news we expected to hear.

Dan gently grabbed my leg as we looked into each other's eyes and realized our hope of being earthly parents was restored. It was another story of renewed hope.

After I gathered myself, my doctor graciously went through where I would be on the high-risk scale, but it was low, since my leaking had decreased. She clearly got the hint through my continued tears that we were going to try and get pregnant.

Even though it would be labeled a high-risk pregnancy, Dan and I both felt comfortable. The words heart failure and death were not words she used to describe the risks. A pregnancy would mean seeing a high-risk doctor, having a few more ultrasounds, and having a few more heart appointments throughout the pregnancy, but it was worth it in our eyes. Their biggest concern was fluid buildup and fatigue, but she believed I could have a normal pregnancy.

After the doctor stepped out, she told the nurse we about fell out of our chairs when she told us we could have our own kids. I just giggled after being told that. Who wouldn't giggle with joy after being told God just performed a miracle in their life?

141

"For my thoughts are not your thoughts, neither are your ways my ways," declares the Lord. "As the heavens are higher than the earth, so are my ways higher than your ways and my thoughts than your thoughts." Isaiah 55:8-9

Believe it or not, the drive home was silent for the first five minutes. We wanted to shout it from the rooftops, but I think we both wondered if that really just happened? We were speechless.

After our feet landed on the ground, we immediately called our parents. They too were just as shocked, but repeatedly said how thankful they were that God chose to answer our years of prayers. What joy it probably brought God's heart for us to make those phone calls. It honestly felt like I was announcing I was pregnant.

After praying in the sanctuary at church just days prior with Bryan, Pastor Steve, and Perry, Dan had to call and share the news with them as well. Each call was received with shouts of praise and amens that I could hear through the other end of the phone. A few minutes after Dan got off the phone with Bryan, Bryan called back. "Dan, did I just hear you correctly or was I dreaming? Did you say that Kristin's heart is strong enough to become pregnant?" Dan reassured him that yes, indeed, God had performed a miracle in my heart.

There was one other person we knew we had to call: Brenda. I will never forget the laughter on the other end of the phone! It brought me back to the laughter we had in Brenda's living room after we found out she was pregnant. We never thought we'd experience that type of laughter again. This was her prayer too, that one day we would have our own child. And we knew we couldn't walk this miraculous journey without her.

After spreading the news about my heart and opening up about it on the blog, many started to ask if I saw a "better" doctor, as opposed to the one I saw in Michigan? I really struggled with that question because, first of all, it diminished God and put Him in this box that we are so good at doing. It diminished His power and healing hand. When something doesn't quite make sense, we chalk it up to something other than God. I understand that as humans we often seek to find answers and logical reasons for events, but sometimes there just are no logical answers.

Was she better because she told us what we wanted to hear? No. If you remember, my previous doctor in Michigan had my test results sent to Mayo Clinic and they gave the exact same answers. Numbers don't lie. My numbers at this past appointment were significantly better than they were before.

Soli Deo Gloria. Glory to God alone.

As we walked into that adult congenital heart office, God knew He would give us the desire of our hearts. Oh, what joy and excitement He probably felt too – waiting to give us that gift.

First though, God needed to do a spiritual heart change in us. It was only fitting that we first had to wrestle with that verse from Psalm 37. Before, I wasn't willing to fully delight myself in the Lord because I was disagreeing with the journey He had taken us down. I felt we should've had kids sooner. I wished our twins were with us. I wanted things to go my way, in my timing, and without pain. I was finally learning to let go and follow God's dream for our life.

It wasn't a mistake that Dan gave the message he did that Wednesday night at youth group. It was all part of God's perfect plan.

And all part of the story.

CHAPTER 18

Praying For New Life

We decided to wait one month before trying to conceive because we wanted to make sure that having a child was what God wanted for us. Yes, we were given the okay, but we wanted to make certain that it was God's will too. We didn't want to have kids just because we could.

Meanwhile, I had a CT scan to ensure that the left coronary artery connection was still in good shape from my surgery in 2001. My doctor must've assumed all would be good because she had already switched my heart medication to pills that were safe to take while pregnant. So we also assumed the scan would only confirm the clearance to get pregnant.

As expected, the CT scan showed that the connection looked great and my doctor gave us her blessing, once more, for me to get pregnant. We basically relived the joy of finding out we could have kids all over again!

Dan often said that God brought us to Minnesota for a healing of the heart. He always just meant our emotional and spiritual hearts, but now that "heart" also included my physical heart.

This heart healing was a miracle that gave us the opportunity to dream of having our own children again; though I found myself still hesitating to dream. We learned with the twins that it was hard to balance dreaming about children, but still taking it one day at a time. I finally succumbed to the fact that we just had to learn to let go of the fears. Again.

Reopening our hearts and minds to the idea of children, resurfaced grief and memories of losing our first two. Dreaming reminded us that life was fragile, and from the beginning, we had to give that child to the Lord.

Slowly we learned to let go, dream about what we would name the baby, who the baby would look like, how tall he or she would be, and how we would parent.

They felt like big dreams, even though I wasn't even pregnant yet, but dreams we couldn't wait to hopefully see come true.

By the beginning of July, I thought that maybe, just MAYBE, I was pregnant. I was starting to feel tired and didn't feel quite like myself.

I wanted to buy the store out of pregnancy tests, wanting to be sure, but I spared the store and cashier and only bought three.

I thought it'd be fun to take one. Why not, right? It was about two days early, so unfortunately it was negative.

The night before I took the second pregnancy test, I struggled to fall asleep because I knew the next day, I could possibly find out if I was pregnant. So that Sunday morning, July 6, 2014, I woke up early with nerves, emotions, and excitement firing on all ends.

I waited the recommended time suggested on the pregnancy test box and to my delight and complete shock, there was a faint pink line.

I immediately ran into the bedroom, woke Dan up and whispered...

"I think I'm pregnant!"

He rubbed the sleep from his eyes and then they became the size of saucers when I showed him the test. We sat there on the edge of the bed trying to comprehend if this was really happening. Was I seriously pregnant? After our initial joy and giddiness, we decided that since the line was rather faint, I should take the last test the next morning. So we spent the rest of the day dreaming.

That afternoon, we took our fishing boat that we completely refurbished, out to a local lake to go fishing. We didn't fish a whole lot, but instead just laid on the boat deck dreaming about what it'd be like to have a little one to fish with. All of the hooks that we'd have to bait, and all of the lines we'd have to untangle. We laid there just imagining the fun times we'd have as a family out on the boat, and opportunities we'd have to teach a child about life. A moment we'll never forget.

Monday morning rolled around and of course I woke up a little early, excited to take my third and final pregnancy test. Who knew the short nights of sleep would start so soon?

Clear as day, I WAS PREGNANT!

This time I decided to wait until Dan woke up, why, I don't know; but when I heard him stirring, I rushed into the room and said, "Good morning baby Daddy!"

His face was priceless. He had the cutest smile as his eyes lit up. The room filled with cheers of joy, hugs, and fighting back tears, as we stared at the results.

Could it REALLY be true? Was there really a BABY inside of me?

I walked into the bathroom at least 10 times to reread the test that morning (no exaggeration) to see if it changed. Dan also kept checking "just to make sure." We sat on the couch that morning and continued dreaming. Did our YEARS of prayers come true again? Dan then confessed to me that he felt like we'd someday have our own, but didn't verbalize it to me (because he knew it hurt and knew there was no possible way). Until that morning. For too many years it was inconceivable, but now life was conceived.

After realizing the pregnancy test wasn't changing, we wondered what we were supposed to do next. We'd never been down this road before, so we went back to what we did after finding out I could get pregnant.

We called our parents.

Many wait until the 12-week mark and especially after the initial doctor's appointment, but it was too much of a miracle and such an answer to prayer that we had to share the news with them. We knew it was trendy to find unique ways to share the news about being pregnant, but we didn't want to take the time to be creative.

We felt the situation in and of itself was inspiring, so no additional creativity was needed.

As we shared the news with them, tears and shrieks of joy filled our phone lines.

Oh, to say the words, "I AM PREGNANT." I relived that moment in my thoughts for weeks after.

What encouragement those words brought to my faith and so it only seemed fitting to read Psalm 139. The words of that Psalm became so tangible and real. God knew this baby would be formed in me, even before WE were born. He knew that child would be a gift like no other.

Only God could rescue fallen dreams and make them whole again.

Because I thought I was going crazy, the day after the positive pregnancy test, I decided to get a confirmation from my doctor. Lo and behold, the first words out of the physician's assistant's mouth were, "You are pregnant! Congratulations!" I could've cried. She asked if it was our first time trying and I said, "Well yes, but..." For some reason I felt compelled to share our journey because it wasn't only our story, but God's story to tell. After telling her a very abbreviated version, she added that she was a believer too, as we both teared up. I told her I just couldn't tell that story without talking about God.

My due date was set for March 17, 2015. (Yes, that would also be St. Patrick's Day and no, we do not have a lick of Irish in us).

Dan and I then had to decide when to tell the rest of the world that I was pregnant. We figured if God created this little life, we wanted to celebrate that life no matter how small the baby was. That child was part of our family, just like our other two babies were, even though they were only three-week-old embryos when they went home to Heaven. If God wanted to call this little one home, it would still be a life to celebrate and a life we would always love. So why not spread the news? Why keep silent what God had done?

So that day, we took a picture of an ice fishing rod (since that's the smallest we had) in between two of our fishing rods. We then announced via Facebook and the blog that were gaining a new fishing buddy come March 2015.

One morning during week seven of my pregnancy, I woke up not feeling well. I felt nauseous and sick (more than normal). I thought GREAT (in a positive sense) since I always wanted to feel symptoms of being pregnant. I wanted to know that my body was responding to a human growing inside of it and symptoms, to me, were a gentle nudge from God that He created a miracle in me.

As noon rolled around, I started to feel crampy and began to see spots of blood. That was the first time I had spotted during the pregnancy, and along with some other symptoms, it caused me to be very concerned. Okay, not concerned, but literally scared.

The memories of the past were all too fresh. The memories of that phone call from Brenda that Monday night, replayed in my mind. I went on a walk, hoping the cramping would go away, but it didn't. It only got worse. I immediately called my doctor when I got home and of course, they were at lunch. So for the next half hour I just cried, read my Bible, and prayed with tears of utter helplessness, that God would spare his/her life.

The nurse finally called back and asked more about my symptoms. I could tell by her voice that she was alarmed. She said she would talk to the doctor to see what she recommended and then call me back. I called Dan to let him know what was going on, or rather the fact that I didn't know what was going on. We were both beside ourselves. Why *again*?

After the nurse had spoken with the doctor, she called back and said I needed to come in for an ultrasound; soon. I was actually hoping they'd recommend an ultrasound, but the other part of me was concerned because they were trying to get me in as early as they could. Did I really miscarry? How could this be happening? I couldn't bear the thought of grieving the loss of another child.

Unfortunately the clinic didn't have openings until 7:30 a.m. the next day, but the nurse suggested the hospital instead. I told her that for my peace of mind, I needed to come in that day. The nurse completely understood and I was able to get in 50 minutes later. Dan worked in the same town as the nearest hospital, so I called him again to let him know that I'd pick him up so we could head straight to the hospital together.

I'd love to say that we had a faith that could move mountains in all of this, but we didn't. We were both in shambles.

We both knew in our hearts that if God had taken this precious life to be with Him, that He would help us get through it, but in our heads we couldn't even fathom the thought. Before opening our car doors to walk in, we sat with hands held together, praying. Praying that God would show us a picture of a healthy baby inside and not of an empty screen like the last time we saw an ultrasound with Tim and Brenda.

Thankfully it was quiet at the hospital so we headed to registration right away. We didn't want to see anybody we knew because we were milliseconds from losing it. We were on the brink of

151

tears - one word about our baby and we would've lost it. Just as our luck would have it, walking to the elevator we ran into someone we knew. Say hi, be polite, but just keep walking.

We sat down for 30 seconds in the waiting room and the technician called us back. He started off by saying that because I was only seven weeks along, that he might not see anything through the abdomen because the baby was so small. I became even more panicked, but at the same time, it was the right thing for him to tell us.

As he rolled the ultrasound probe across my stomach, I could see a black hole. Almost immediately he calmly said, "I think there's the baby!" I lifted my head up ever so slightly to look into Dan's eyes that were welled up with tears. Mine joined his. Then a few seconds later, "And there is the flickering heartbeat!"

I was trying to hold it together, but just couldn't anymore. The peace of God that said, "My child, everything will be okay," overwhelmed me. For the next few minutes, I just had tears streaming, trying to keep as still as I could so the technician could get the best looks at this little miracle as he could.

I kept apologizing to him for crying, but he said that life really is a miracle and that since this was our first one, it probably meant a lot. I quietly told him that we'd actually been in this position before, but in a different way, and we had seen an empty screen. So to see a little life, all I could do was cry. He completely understood.

That little baby, whose tiny hands and feet weren't even formed yet, had the heartbeat that screamed, "Yes, I am alive! Here I am!" And that was what I wanted my faith to look like too. I want my heart to be so in charge of my body - a heart full of God and faith that it overtakes who I am. THAT is what we saw in our little baby that day.

The technician confirmed that we had a healthy baby thus far, measuring right on (should be 1 centimeter – our little baby was 1.1) with a heartbeat of 142.

God intended that whole ordeal for good, as He always does, because that is what He promises. (Romans 8:28). But even if we would've lost that baby, we knew God would've used that for good because He is in the business of redeeming the broken. In this situation, the reality of another possible miscarriage ended up being a gift because we received the gift of pictures. Pictures were what we didn't have with our first two. We dreamed of one day holding ultrasound pictures and now that day finally came. They were pictures filled with so much life and so much hope. Pictures that reminded us that God CAN move mountains, even when my faith cannot.

Typically, ultrasounds don't happen at seven weeks - they are usually between 10 to 12 weeks. But God's plan was much better than ours because we were reassured that even at seven weeks, there was still life inside and, indeed, I was still pregnant.

So why was I having symptoms of a miscarriage? The nurse practitioner called me about an hour later and said they were unsure why the symptoms presented themselves the way they did, but to just take it easy the rest of the day. I would have no problem doing so because then I had an excuse to just sit and stare at those ultrasound pictures of our sweet baby.

As a blogger, one thing that comes quite easily for me, most of the time, are words. It's not very often that I am speechless.

Though, one thing I actually found difficult to talk about was being pregnant.

You would think talking about the very thing we wanted for so many years would be easy, but we knew all too well the pain other couples felt of not being able to have a child and not being able to become pregnant. Yet, there I sat, carrying a child. So I struggled to talk about my pregnancy because I didn't want to cause pain for other couples who were experiencing the same pain we had once felt.

We knew the pain of being on the outside, hearing the word "congratulations" spoken to someone who just found out they were expecting. We knew the pain of hearing other couples talk about trying to get pregnant and the excitement surrounding it. We knew the pain of listening to others talk about dreams of parenting, buying baby clothes, celebrating birthdays, and creating a family, all while we weren't able to do the same.

And now we were those people having those same conversations. The same conversations we so desperately wanted for so long and now had. Because of our past, because of the grief journey we had been on, our perspective was different. Because of the losses, we could now see a deeper beauty.

If we hadn't experienced loss first, we wouldn't have understood the depth of love we could have for a child. We wouldn't have understood the power of an ultrasound where we COULD see a beating heart, if we hadn't first seen a blank screen. We wouldn't have understood the intricacies of what God does in knitting together a child, if it wasn't for the IVF process. To follow a pregnancy that closely with Brenda, we wouldn't have been able to fathom the miracle of having our own. If it weren't for God's gift of those two little babies, our hearts wouldn't have been as full as they were when I was pregnant. We just had to be patient and wait for God to make something beautiful out of the loss.

Sometimes it takes experiencing the difficult in life and even experiencing loss, to understand the joy of the present. God used our little baby inside of me to give us new hope. To remind us of where we had been. To remind us that God's promises do hold true.

Dan and I decided to take a babymoon, which is the trip expecting parents take to have one last hurrah before the baby comes. We fell in love with the Florida Keys after we had vacationed there the previous April, so we knew it'd be our destination of choice once again. Unfortunately, it rained six out of the eight days we were there, as a tropical storm passed through, but of course that didn't stop us from having fun and making the most of our trip before we became a family of three.

It was on that trip that I was able to experience "the looks." You know, those quick glances that people give you - not in your eyes, but at your stomach. The night we arrived at the condo we were renting for the week, we rode the elevator with two elderly women. As we stepped off and the doors were closing, I overheard one of the women whisper to the other, "I think she's pregnant!"

I loved the fact that people first looked at my growing stomach and then at my face. To hear the words, "Congratulations, when are you due?" was a comment and question I longed to be asked and now was finally happening. While in the Keys we went on a snorkeling trip, and as we climbed aboard the boat to head out to the reef, the captain looked at my stomach and with a sly grin he asked, "What happened to you?" Wearing a swimsuit made it pretty obvious that I was pregnant. Men have some of the strangest ways of saying congratulations, but I loved it. I loved being pregnant and having people notice.

About a week after we arrived home from our trip, we had the gender-revealing ultrasound. At first we were thinking it was a boy and we always pictured ourselves having a boy for some reason; so we were a bit surprised to hear the doctor say that it was a GIRL! Though of course we couldn't have been more thrilled! The doctor assured us that he was pretty sure it was a girl, so we could go out and buy one pink item. So of course Dan and I bought a pink fishing rod on the way home.

Speaking of tests, my OB doctor was concerned that our baby would be born with the same congenital heart disease I had, and didn't feel comfortable delivering our baby girl if she did. Since our local hospital didn't have doctors that could care for a newborn with a heart defect, that meant I'd have to go to Minneapolis, which was 2 hours away, to deliver her. He decided to order a fetal ECHO, where they're able to take an intricate look at each chamber of the heart, all through an ultrasound-type test. During that 1 ½ hour test, we were able to see the inner workings of our baby girl's heart and it was incredible. I was in awe of how a machine could get that close of an image of our baby's heart. We knew from previous genetic testing that there was very little chance of passing on my heart defect, so we weren't surprised when the test showed that she had a perfectly normal functioning heart, at only four months gestation.

I also had a few more heart tests to see if the pregnancy was affecting the function and rhythm of my own heart. A month before my due date, I had my last heart ECHO and though there was a little more regurgitation in the mitral valve, the doctor said that if she looked at just my face, she wouldn't have guessed that I was pregnant. My heart medication was doing what it was supposed to be doing, by keeping my blood pressure low and keeping my heart in rhythm. What a miracle, really.

The thing was, the big concern over me being pregnant wasn't the delivery, but the nine months of strain that my heart would be under in carrying a baby. Even though the ECHO showed there was just a little more leakage, my cardiologist wasn't concerned at all and even said that I could have a normal delivery without needing any additional medications or machines. And I didn't have to deliver in Minneapolis.

As much as we were willing to do whatever it took to have a healthy baby and a healthy delivery, we were praying that we wouldn't have to travel two hours to have our baby girl. It was hard enough experiencing the pregnancy without family around, since our families were in Michigan, but we were given the gift of friends who were like family to us. So we were glad that at least we could deliver our little girl in town and share the experience with our friends close by.

Dan and I are pretty open people and we do not keep secrets well. If you know us personally, you'd probably agree! One thing we DID keep secret though, except with close friends and family, was the appointment I had on Friday, March 13, 2015.

At that appointment, my doctor said that if the baby didn't come during the weekend, that I should come in that Tuesday, March 17, on her due date. Even though we were praying she'd come that weekend, we at least knew she'd be born within the week. Finally our dreams of holding our little girl were getting closer!

The day after that appointment, March 14, I was starting to think that "the day" was coming. That night we were at a friend's house and I started to have some contractions. Nothing real earth-shattering, but contractions nonetheless. I went to bed wondering if that night would be our last night as a family of two.

Well, I woke up Sunday morning not feeling the greatest, but at the last minute, decided to go to church. As the day progressed, I started to feel better, which actually made me frustrated because I just wanted to have her. And then of course Monday rolled around with no contractions.

I just kept coming back to Proverbs 16:9 which says, "In their hearts humans plan their course, but the Lord establishes their steps." If I truly believed that He would establish our steps, then why was I not letting Him? I guess our arms were just so ready to love that little girl, so I pleaded with God to help her come soon!

It was less than an hour later, after my plea to God that Monday morning, when my doctor's office called. The nurse said there was an opening Tuesday morning at the hospital and that my doctor wanted me to come in Monday afternoon to get a catheter put in; this was a device I needed in case I wasn't dilated. Of course, I was elated! I right away called Dan and told him that tomorrow we were going to be parents!

I spent the rest of the day nesting, you know, getting the last load of laundry done, cleaning out the leftovers in the refrigerator, getting my bag packed, and of course, doing things that really didn't need to be done, but wanted to do, to pass time.

That Monday afternoon we headed to the doctor to see if I was dilated. When my doctor first mentioned the catheter, you could tell it wasn't his favorite thing to do to a patient, so we were praying that I could walk away from that appointment without one.

To our surprise he said, "I see no need for a catheter because you are dilated to a 3!" As I closed my eyes and did a little pump with my fist, my plea became a prayer of relief and thanksgiving to God.

I went to bed that night with scenarios playing through my head, as I pictured our family of three in the hospital room. Dreaming of what it'd be like to give birth. Seeing her face for the first time. A face filled with so much hope, promise, and grace. To hold and gently caress her body. To wipe away my own tears, realizing our years of prayers were being answered through this tiny little baby.

Every time I woke up that night, I put my hand on my stomach, taking in every last bit of her inside of me.

CHAPTER 19

Amazing Grace

We were told to come in at 5:00 a.m. on Tuesday, March 17, 2015, but to call the labor and delivery floor an hour before, just in case the nurses were short-staffed or the rooms were full. Sure enough, when I called at 3:50 a.m., they were busy and short-staffed (which I completely understood, but did NOT want to hear), and they asked that we come in at 7:00 a.m. instead. The dear nurse told me to go back to bed if I could, to get a few more hours of sleep. Yeah right! Sleep is highly overrated when you know you are about to give birth to your first child! I tried, but not a chance.

Even though I was ready to rock and roll, I was glad I could wait at home, rather than at the hospital. So I took my time, thinking about what the day would hold, took a shower, got ready, and finished packing our bags. I called one more time before we left, just to make sure that 7:00 was still a good time for us to come. The nurse gave us the okay, so off we went to have a baby.

160

As Dan and I drove to the hospital, with an empty car seat strapped in the back, there was a stunning sunrise that God had painted for us as we reflected on the fact that it was the last car ride together as a family of two. We had fallen in love with her for nine months, and just couldn't wait to meet her face to face. As we made our way, I wasn't sure if it was nerves or what, but I started to feel some cramping. I was hoping it was just a small reminder that she was alive and well.

On that drive, Dan and I also had to have a hard, but real conversation. What if I didn't make it? What if there were complications and Dan would be left to raise our baby girl alone? It maybe wasn't a conversation that most have on the way to the hospital, but I am thankful we had that candid talk.

If God decided to take me to my eternal home, Dan said, "You take care of our two babies in Heaven and tell them that Daddy loves them, and I will take care of our little girl here, and remind her every day that Mommy loves her so much."

Then I said my part. As hard as it was to say, I encouraged Dan to find someone to marry for his sake, but also so our daughter would have a mommy. It was a conversation we needed to have, but a conversation we prayed would not become a reality. And a conversation we hoped to never have again.

We were escorted up to the labor and delivery floor and were met by a wonderful nurse, Jody. As she led us to our room, it almost felt like we were at a conference or special event, as we were led from one place to another, meeting new people here and there. As Dan set up our home, I was immediately started on IV fluids, received Pitocin to get the contractions going, had my blood drawn, was put on a baby heart monitor, and a contraction monitor.

Remember those cramps I was feeling on the way to the hospital? Well, when my nurse hooked me up to the contraction monitor, she asked if I knew I was contracting already. Who knew?

The first few hours were spent hanging out in a hospital room, just waiting and waiting. Dan and I got a game of Skip-Bo in and took a few laps around the labor and delivery floor.

By about 10:00 a.m., the contractions were getting stronger and stronger; so at 10:30, the anesthesiologist came in to start the epidural. After a few seconds, I could feel the epidural moving down into my legs and all I remember saying was, "This stuff is AMAZING!" I have to say that I do have a fairly high pain tolerance, though I suppose everyone thinks that of themselves; but if there was a med that could lessen the pain of a beautiful process, I was willing to take it. I had nothing to prove. Plus, the doctor recommended I get one because he wanted to keep my heart rate down. Then soon after, I started to feel pretty sleepy and was able to rest.

It was still slow going, but finally the moment came when I realized she was coming! The nurse checked me and sure enough, I was fully dilated and it was time. My doctor thought it would be about 7:00 before I would start pushing, so he quickly ran home to grab some supper; but my nurse had him turn right around because she also knew it was time. It was now 6:00 and once my doctor returned, it was show time. What had previously been a quiet hospital room became a flurry of activity. Nurses came out of the woodwork, flooding into the delivery room, turning on different monitors, prepping towels, and flipping on the warming light over the baby's bed. It felt like a big party was about to get started.

The doctor was a little concerned that I'd push myself too far, so he told me to be sure to take breaths when needed, for my heart's sake. We hadn't been able to attend any birthing classes because they were all on basketball nights (I was coaching JV girls basketball for

162

our local Christian school at the time), but looking back, I am so glad we didn't. It was a unique experience to us and we didn't go into that day with any expectations - especially when it came to the delivery.

At 6:52 p.m., our little miracle of 8 pounds, 2 ounces, and 22 inches long, named Mazy Grace Sterk, was born!

She let out a big wail and the doctor confirmed, "She sure has a good set of lungs on her!" I remember seeing her face for the first time and realizing that I was seconds away from holding our precious child. A child I carried for nine months and now gave birth to naturally. A true miracle was right before me. I looked over at Dan who had succumbed to tears. As they gently placed her on my chest, I was so overwhelmed with emotion. Tears streamed as our hearts fell in love with this baby that we now got to hold. We couldn't believe that Mazy Grace was finally here and so perfect. Seeing those beautiful bright eyes, long skinny legs, her ten toes and fingers, for the first time, oh the joy that filled our hearts. So many emotions, dreams, and love wrapped up in one little baby.

After the nurses cleaned her off, they placed her on my chest. We were finally a family of three. Dan looked into my eyes and said, "She is beautiful, just like her mom."

It must've been only 15 minutes after Mazy was born and Dan had already slipped out of the delivery room. A nurse came in with bracelets for Dan and me to prove that we were the parents, and asked where Dan was. I wasn't sure and didn't even realize that he had left to be honest! I was too enamored with staring at my precious little girl wrapped in my arms. Dan had escaped to the lobby to call our parents, family, and friends, to share the news that Mazy Grace had been born. He was just so excited that he couldn't wait to tell everyone! Like I said, we can't keep secrets!

The rest of the night was a bit of a blur. There was much to learn, like how to give Mazy a bath, breastfeed, and care for her; but what came naturally was loving her. That night as we were getting ready for bed, we just stared at her as tears continued to make paths down our cheeks. So many emotions wrapped up in one tiny bundle. I didn't want that day to end.

Now the story behind her name. Days after finding out I could get pregnant, we started to talk about names. Meanwhile, when Dan's parents were visiting us in Minnesota, his mom had mentioned that she knew a friend of a friend, and down the line, who had named their daughter Mazy Grace. When she had said that name, I thought, "That's it!" I poked Dan and whispered, "I LOVE that name!" He thought it was kind of weird, but I liked the so-called "different" names, where he was more traditional.

We let it rest for a while, and a week or two later, we talked about names again. We knew we wanted a name that defined what God had done, a name that held meaning, and a name that described our story in some way.

The word that we kept coming back to was GRACE. God's AMAZING GRACE.

It was clear and it only seemed right to name our child, Mazy Grace. Though that meant we'd also have to have a girl. Well, God knew that our child was meant to be named Mazy Grace because sure enough, a girl was exactly what we had! She was tangible evidence of God's undeniable and amazing grace in our lives.

2 Corinthians 12:9 declares: "My grace is sufficient for you, for my power is made perfect in weakness."

After having Mazy, it was a trying time. But grace isn't just for the tough times, even though it's in our weakness where God shows His strength. Grace is always there to envelop us in the good times and the bad, as long as we are ready and willing to fall into His arms of grace.

The next day flew by quickly with visitors coming and showing their love to little Mazy throughout the day. What a blessing it was to have the family of God walk alongside us not only that day, but throughout the entire pregnancy. That day though, I felt just a little off. I figured that could be assumed, especially after giving birth, right?

While being prepped to have Mazy, I was pumped with IV fluids, which is a normal procedure. It is common to retain some fluid before and after delivery, and eventually the body passes all of the excess fluid. We didn't realize it at the time, but my body wasn't doing what a normal woman's body should do after a delivery.

We knew Thursday morning was "going home" day, so we started our morning off slowly. I was extremely tired, which was expected, but I had no appetite and every time I breastfed Mazy, I felt like my heart was going to beat out of my chest. I couldn't lie down to sleep, but had to sit up because otherwise I'd be short of breath. I just assumed those were normal things to experience after giving birth, so I said nothing. Boy was I wrong.

CHAPTER 20

Adjusting To Life At Home

At home that Thursday night, when we sat down to eat supper, I had no appetite. When it came to sleeping, I found myself wheezing and unable to breathe. I propped my pillows up, but that didn't seem to help. The first night home with a newborn typically isn't a good night of sleep anyway, so I just dismissed my inability to catch my breath as exhaustion.

By Friday morning, I knew something was wrong. I called my doctor and they suggested I come in that day to try and diagnose what was going on. I had labs taken and the doctor discovered that my fluid levels, which should've been around 125, were in the 2,000s. My body had retained an incredible amount of fluid and I needed to get rid of it pronto, for fear of what it could do to my heart.

Meanwhile, as I was sitting in the exam room waiting to hear the test results, I could hear Mazy crying out in the lobby. Even at just a couple of days old, I had already learned her distinct cry. But that meant Dan had to try and give Mazy a bottle with formula, and I never showed him how. After a few nurses and even a doctor offered their help (which he kindly declined), he fed Mazy her first bottle. Nothing like getting thrown into fatherhood!

The doctor prescribed a diuretic to help pass the excessive amount of fluid I had and said I would be in the bathroom all night. Unfortunately though, I experienced quite the opposite. I barely went and started to feel sicker and sicker.

By 6:30 a.m. that Saturday, I just couldn't take it anymore. Mazy had hardly slept and I went to Dan in tears, expressing to him that I was not okay. I felt lethargic, couldn't breathe, breastfeeding made my heart feel like it was going to beat out of my chest, and I could barely walk without having to sit down and rest.

While at the doctor's office the day before, the doctor told me that if I didn't start to feel better, I had to go to the ER. The thing was, Mazy was supposed to have a wellness checkup at 9:20 that morning, so I decided to try and hang on until then, and bypass going to the ER.

Thankfully time passed quickly and before we knew it, we were checking into the doctor's office. I told the front desk I needed to be seen as well, as an urgent care patient. The doctor took a quick look at Mazy and she checked out perfectly fine and healthy. Then he asked me what I was feeling. As I described my symptoms and he felt the amount of fluid in my legs, one of the first things he said was, "My goal is to keep you from being admitted into the hospital today." He thought I was carrying around at least five to six pounds of excess fluid in just my legs. Right away he called over to the hospital to see if they could do an emergency or on-demand ECHO. I suppose on-demand was the kinder way of putting it.

We had to wait about 30 minutes for me to have the test, but it was worth it. I knew something was wrong and I couldn't keep living like that. While on the exam table, with the medical technician recording images of my heart, I fell asleep numerous times. I was completely exhausted and my body had had enough. I was trying to recover from having a baby, trying to breastfeed, trying to get SOME sleep, while my heart was working so hard to circulate the excess fluid that had built up. I was depleted.

While we waited for the test results to come in, the doctor ordered a stronger diuretic for me to take. I HAD to get that fluid out of me or I would be hospitalized. When I went to Wal-Mart to pick up my prescription, I was heading to the bathroom when I felt the need to just sit down in the middle of the aisle to rest. I could barely walk through a store. When I got back in the car, I laid my head down, wishing I could just start the past few days over. I was at my end. Physically. Mentally. Emotionally. Could I really go on?

A cardiologist was able to read the results and the doctor called me with the report.

Heart failure.

As he put it, my "pump" looked great, except the left side of my heart was enlarged and the mitral valve was toast (in his words). There was so much fluid built up that my mitral valve couldn't keep up with the overload and had completely failed. The tricuspid valve was also not operating correctly.

He recommended that I have my valve issue taken care of sooner rather than later, but what did that mean? Well, he said I would need open heart surgery within the next week or two.

WHAT? Another surgery now? We knew that having a child could affect my valve, but we just didn't expect this. We were now faced with the possibility of open heart surgery, me trying to recover from giving birth, all while trying to care for a newborn. The next

168

step would be to schedule an appointment with my heart doctor in Minneapolis and get some further testing done. After I hung up the phone, I think I was so sick that I couldn't even fully comprehend the reality that I needed another surgery.

Thankfully my parents were visiting and could help with Mazy, meals, and just be there to support me. They had been down this road of heart complications with me before, though we were a little caught off guard with this news that my heart was failing. Another open heart surgery so soon after having a baby wasn't easy news to swallow. After processing the news with them, my mom wondered aloud that maybe after I passed the fluid, my valves would return to normal functioning. But could my heart wait that long?

Two days after that shocking ECHO, I had an appointment with my primary care physician. After hearing the concern she had for me that weekend, I realized what a serious situation I was in. My heart, that I thought was supposed to do okay with a pregnancy and delivery, was now failing me. The doctor's biggest goal was to ensure that I was passing fluid, so I had to weigh myself every day to make sure I was, and as of that Monday, two days after starting to take that stronger diuretic, I had lost 15 pounds.

Carrying around 15 pounds of excess fluid explained why I had difficulty breathing, felt sluggish, was weak, had a loss of appetite, and was exhausted. When I thought about carrying a 15 lb. weight in a backpack, no wonder I felt a bit off.

By the next day, I had lost 12 more pounds, bringing the total to 27 pounds in three days.

Twenty-seven pounds. I finally saw a bone in my foot that I hadn't seen in over a month. I also had feeling back in my feet and was able to put my wedding rings back on. I was even able to put my slippers on, instead of having to wear Dan's size 12 slippers. Milestones that proved that the medication was finally working.

My primary care physician was able to speak to my cardiologist personally, which was helpful since I spent that day trying to schedule an appointment with her, only to get the answering machine every time. They concluded we needed to wait it out a bit, to see if losing the excess fluid would increase my valve function.

My cardiologist then called me personally, to see if I felt I could wait a few weeks to see if my heart did improve. At the time I felt incredibly fatigued, sick, and completely worn out, but I didn't want to stop fighting. I was willing to try and wait those two weeks to see if my symptoms improved. If I could bypass open heart surgery, I wanted to do what I could.

Mazy was a much needed distraction from the realities of my health situation. We decided that no matter what happened with my heart, we weren't going to let it get us down, but keep pushing forward. Sure enough, over the next two weeks, I started to see small improvements in how I felt, but I wasn't going to get my hopes up just yet.

I made it those two weeks and had my scheduled heart appointment. My cardiologist believed that my mitral valve declined too fast and too suddenly to stop functioning without an outside source affecting it, like the fluid. If you remember, I had a heart appointment a month prior to having Mazy and my valve looked great. That's why my cardiologist believed there was something else that was causing my valve to malfunction.

Before I became pregnant, I had a mild/moderate leaking in that valve. However, after reading the newest test results, she determined that after giving birth to Mazy, I now had moderate/severe leaking of the mitral valve, even after I passed all the fluid. Though the tests also showed that my heart was no longer enlarged, which meant there was slight improvement. It was evident that the fluid did indeed cause my heart to enlarge and my valve to malfunction, but what did that mean for my future?

Now it would just take MORE time to see if my mitral valve would eventually leak less and return to a somewhat normal functioning level, which meant no surgery was needed in the immediate future. We walked away from that appointment knowing my doctor was very optimistic that my valve could return to the condition it was prior to pregnancy; so we too wanted to have that same optimism and believe that God could heal my heart once again.

If I could survive the next few weeks on the diuretic, she believed the weeks would only get easier. I was willing to give it a go.

Both my heart and family doctors kept reminding me to make it my goal to get ME healthy so I could take better care of Mazy. I thought that idea was good in theory, but try telling that to a new mom who was attempting to breastfeed, trying to pass fluids, had a failing heart, and was just trying to stay alive. It was all too much. I knew they were right, but the medication made me even more fatigued and worn out, since I dropped so much weight so quickly.

I finally hit my breaking point and had a meltdown. When things get tough, my response is to put my head down and keep pushing; it's just my personality. The problem was that I ended up wearing myself out, and before I knew it, I was beyond exhausted. So many times, I wondered, "Is this normal?" or "Should I really feel this way?" I realized that recovering from having a baby takes a while in and of itself, but I didn't know it was supposed to be that difficult. Then to have the complications I did, just accentuated it all.

Thankfully we had amazing friends that stepped in and helped on so many levels. Mazy was not a content baby, so there were times when friends would just come over and hold her, while I rested. Then at night we often hung out with our best friends, Matt and Brianna, who happened to live right in town. Then to give me a break, she would just hold and sing Mazy to sleep. The meals they made for us, I could never repay them for. And the sanity they gave us, was just what we needed.

During the next few weeks, I continued to pass fluid. If I gained more than three pounds or if I noticed my ankles swelling, I knew it was time to take the diuretic. Unfortunately, the medication caused fatigue and lightheadedness, but I knew I had to continue to take it to get healthy again.

I thought that after having Mazy I would be in baby bliss, much like after you get married. I don't know about you, but our first year of marriage wasn't necessarily wedded bliss. We sure had a lot of growing to do, so in the same fashion, after having a baby, it's not all cuddles, coos and ahhs.

I vividly remember at one point sitting on our couch in tears, wondering why God was allowing this all to happen during what was supposed to be such a joyful time. A few people told me that the devil was just trying to steal the joy out of having a newborn, and I think they nailed it. I was determined to not let the devil win. When I chose to celebrate small milestones and victories, I was choosing to let God win and not the devil, who just wanted me to doubt and fear.

Problem was, I still found myself thinking I was failing on every level.

I felt I was failing as a mother. I was unable to breastfeed due to the effects the diuretic had on my milk supply and I couldn't calm my own child. I would do everything in my power to try and get Mazy to stop crying, but she just continued to cry. And cry. And I felt like I was failing.

I took Mazy in for a routine appointment and the medical professional asked if I ever had her checked for acid reflux. Every time Mazy ate, she would spit up. I'm not just talking about a little dribble, but enough to create a large puddle in the burp cloth in my hand. I didn't think much of it at the time, but occasionally she screamed when I fed her as well. I thought she just didn't want to eat, but she would eat a little bit, then scream. Eat a little, then scream. I sat her up to burp and it seemed like it would all just come back up. It was an extremely frustrating scenario that continued to play out day after day, feeding after feeding.

After realizing that maybe acid reflux was the issue, the doctor put her on a medication and, lo and behold, that helped incredibly. The screaming stopped during feedings. The spitting up was just as much, but she didn't cry each time she did. I finally found an answer to something.

After the first three months, Dan and I both looked at each other and thought, "Was 'this' how parenting was supposed to be?" I was constantly in tears, not knowing what or where I needed help. Dan would help, but in my mind, it was never good enough. I needed more - but I didn't know what that "more" was. It was a spiral of emotions and I was sinking deeper and deeper.

We concluded that I had needs that he just couldn't fill. It wasn't something wrong with him, but had everything to do with my health and Mazy's struggles. It all became too much for me at one time.

Mazy was also not sleeping well because of the acid reflux, which made me more emotional and exhausted. Of course, I had it in my head that I'd get Mazy to sleep through the night by month three or four because that's what the books said was possible. Well, month three came and left, and she was still waking up several times a night. I, again, felt like I was failing. By month five, she was still sleeping in her bouncy seat to help with the reflux, was consistently waking up multiple times a night, and there seemed to be no end.

Looking back, I was clearly dealing with some postpartum depression. I was at a loss and so was Dan.

One night we finally went on a date, just the two of us. It was then that we hashed it all out and we both turned a corner. When we sat down, we both humbly expressed that we weren't going to try and defend ourselves, but listen to the other with open ears and hearts. And thus began a new chapter. After that crucial date, our marriage started to improve, and I was starting to feel a bit better too. Dan was able to calm Mazy down (where before she only wanted mom), which gave me a much needed break, and we felt like a family who was going to make it.

Despite the changes though, the damage was already done for me personally. I had lost myself and didn't know who I was. Everything about me seemed unfamiliar. I so deeply wanted Mazy to know she was safe and sound. I wanted her to feel the love I had for her, but it seemed like I always came up short. I so deeply wanted to be the best mom, but what was I doing wrong?

But that exact thought was part of the problem in and of itself...

I was doing nothing wrong. God had a much bigger plan in store for us, even through those difficult months. As Brenda gently reminded me one day amid all the struggles - God sees, God knows, God hears. God knew our heart's desires. He knew Mazy struggled. Even though our prayers weren't answered in the timeframe we thought they should've been, God still had a plan.

CHAPTER 21

God's Perfect Timing

"For the Lord is good and his love endures forever; his faithfulness continues through all generations." Psalm 100:5

Six months had passed since Mazy was born and I was scheduled to go in for another heart checkup. Sadly, we knew going into the appointment that my heart still wasn't functioning as it should. My exercise tolerance wasn't what it once was and even though fatigue is a symptom of being a new mom, I knew by the level that I felt fatigued, that it was a definite symptom of heart failure.

At the appointment, the technician shockingly said, "I read you had ALCAPA (the reason I needed open heart surgery when I was 17) and that you had a child." She wasn't quite sure what to say. I couldn't help but share about God's goodness and the miracle that Mazy Grace really was. God chose to heal my heart and allow me to have such a wonderful pregnancy, despite my medical history.

After my heart ECHO, EKG, and labs, it was determined that my heart wasn't where it should be and where they were hoping it'd be after six months. On the plus side though, open heart surgery wasn't on the horizon just yet. My heart did have irregular beats, but the doctor hoped that with more time, things would return to normal.

The rest of the year seemed to fly by as we started to adjust to a new normal. Life as new parents started to become easier. Then in May 2016, over a year after having Mazy, I had another routine heart checkup. Two weeks prior, I had an MRI of my heart to get a baseline of where my heart was, in case I needed open heart surgery. It was a long MRI, since my heart wasn't beating at a consistent pace, making quality images hard to get. After two hours, it was finally complete.

While waiting to hear the results that day, I was nervous. Would today be the day I needed to prepare myself to hear the words "open heart surgery" again?

The nurse finally called us back to get the results. The doctor observed that at some point in my life, I had a mild heart attack, which quite possibly could've occurred even before my first open heart surgery. She again commented how amazing it was that I lived until 17, considering the condition of my heart. As she pondered over that thought, I couldn't help but say, "It really was a miracle." God was the one who sustained my heart - not me.

The MRI showed my mitral valve, the valve that my doctor assumed would require surgery in the near future, was only MILDLY leaking. The very valve that a year ago was "completely toast" as one doctor called it, was leaking LESS than when I was given the green light to get pregnant! My leak did not heal on its own - it was God and God alone. Another miracle.

My doctor gave us the green light to get pregnant *again*, though this time I'd have to be monitored more closely if we chose to do so. I'd also have to deliver in Minneapolis, since my local high-risk doctor said he wouldn't feel comfortable delivering another baby for me, for fear of my heart failing.

One part of me wanted to get pregnant right away and capitalize on the health that God had given me, but as we prayed, we realized God was calling us to quite the opposite. God was giving us a spirit of contentment as a family of three. Though my heart was getting better, we knew there was a likely chance that we'd go through the same ordeal with it failing again. And if it did, would I ever recover? Was that something we really wanted to go through a second time?

In thinking about God's perfect timing and perfect ways, I can't help but think about this verse from James 1:17 - "Every good and perfect gift is from above, coming down from the Father of the heavenly lights, who does not change like shifting shadows."

I find it to be no coincidence, but a God-cidence, that God has used the number 17 to have significance in our life. The more I have become aware of numbers in the Bible and the meaning behind them, the more I have learned that God can work and show Himself to be omnipotent and omniscient through something as simple as numbers.

At the age of 17, I found out I had a congenital heart condition.
On January 17, 2001, I had open heart surgery.

178

On January 17, 2011, Brenda met with the Fertility Clinic for the first
　　time to talk about being a gestational carrier.
On September 17, 2012, God took our babies home to be with Him.
On May 17, 2013, our two little babies were due.
On March 17, 2015, our little girl, Mazy Grace was born.
And in 2017, there were BIG changes up ahead...

When Dan and I were in college, Dan roomed with our friend,
Shaun. Shaun was the friend who had called me on the phone to tell
me I was crazy because Dan was trying to take me out to dinner and
in my naiveté had said, "No, I already ate." Shaun was in the pre-
seminary track, working toward becoming a pastor. Dan and Shaun
often joked about how awesome it would be to do ministry in the
same church; Shaun as the senior pastor and Dan as the youth pastor.

Over the years, Dan had always told me that there were two
pastors who, if they ever called and said they needed a youth pastor,
he'd jump at the opportunity. Well, Shaun called that summer of
2016 and said his church was looking for a youth pastor.

At the time though, we weren't looking to leave Minnesota
and our youth group kids just yet. We knew we eventually wanted to
land back in Michigan closer to family, but just not yet. In our minds,
we were committed to being in Minnesota for at least four years, and
we had only been there for three. So Dan told Shaun that even
though he'd love the opportunity to work with him, and even
though Shaun's church was literally down the road from my parents,
the timing wasn't right. To our amazement, Shaun replied, "We
aren't looking to fill this position until next year anyway."

Over the next couple of months, Dan worked on putting his résumé together and sent it off to Shaun's church. Two months later, the head of the search committee called and asked if we could come for an interview. So we packed our bags for a whirlwind weekend and boarded a plane for a quick flight to Michigan.

A week later, Dan was offered the position, and we decided to accept it. Not only was Dan going to be working with his old college roommate in a town we could see ourselves settling down in, but we were also moving back to the area I grew up in. You can imagine how much excitement I had! After Mazy was born, all I wanted to do was move back to Michigan. As I was dealing with my heart issues and a newborn at the same time, I just wanted to be by family. In hindsight though, I'm so glad Dan didn't listen to my persistent pleas. God's plan was worth the wait! I learned to rely on my friends out in Minnesota, who quickly became not only my best friends, but my family.

And then the reality of moving to Michigan set in. We had to find a new house, in a new town, and we had to start packing up our belongings. When we moved to Minnesota, it was just Dan and me. Now we had a two-year-old and all the extra furniture, clothes, and toys that go along.

Probably the hardest part, the part we were least prepared for, was leaving the friends that had become family to us in Minnesota. Friends who walked through the pain of an ugly separation from our previous church, friends who cried with us in dealing with the loss of our first two babies, friends who covered us in prayer for the healing of my heart, and friends who adopted us as part of their families and even invited us over for holidays and birthdays. We were excited about moving closer to our immediate families, but we mourned leaving the new extended family that we had come to love. During those last few weeks, I spent many of those days in tears, grieving what we were going to leave behind. I knew we were meant to move, but driving away that last day was so hard.

A few weeks prior to moving in May 2017, I had my routine heart checkup. It was then that we learned another open heart surgery was just around the corner. I was wheezing and had a harder time breathing while lying flat, but I honestly thought it was just allergies. Ha! That mildly leaking valve had turned to severely leaking in a year's time. The news was still hard to hear, but at the same time, oddly relieving. For years I'd been told I would need another surgery, so at every appointment, we wondered if this would be the year. Finally the suspense was over and we had an answer. It would be within the year.

My doctor in Minnesota referred me to a former colleague of hers at the University of Michigan in Ann Arbor. Soon after moving, we met with my new cardiologist and after speaking with her briefly, she agreed it was time to address my valve issue surgically. She referred me to Dr. Bolling, who wasn't only the University of Michigan's top surgeon for mitral valve repairs, but also one of the best in the world.

Dr. Bolling was a popular man, which meant scheduling an appointment with him was difficult. We finally met with him in late August and scheduled surgery for November 30, 2017. Dr. Bolling was confident that he could *repair* my valve. Up until that point, every doctor we consulted thought it would be a valve *replacement*. When surgeons do a replacement, they either use a tissue valve from an animal or a mechanical valve. To us, neither option was great. A tissue valve lasts only 10 to 15 years before it has to be replaced. With a mechanical valve, you have to be on blood thinners for the rest of your life. So anytime you got the slightest cut on your finger, it would be hard to stop the bleeding.

So when Dr. Bolling said he was confident he could repair the valve, we were ecstatic! Every nurse we talked to from then on said, "If anyone can repair your valve, Dr. Bolling can." When it came to mitral valve repair, Dr. Bolling was the expert. Let me put this in perspective. In the U.S., the average number of mitral valve repairs a surgeon performs is five per year. That means a surgeon does about 150 surgeries in their career. Dr. Bolling has performed more than 4,000 mitral valve surgeries to date. In the U.S., while the success rate for mitral valve repair is 41 percent, the repair rate for the surgeons at the University of Michigan as a whole, is more than 95 percent.[12] We left that first meeting excited and at peace. We knew I was going to be in the best hands possible.

Despite our excitement over just needing a repair, November 30th sure seemed far away; could I make it until then? By September, I was getting weekly blood draws to check how much fluid I was retaining. I was also struggling to do everyday tasks such as going up and down the stairs to do laundry and carry Mazy when she wanted to be held. It was even difficult to do something as simple as grocery shopping. My heart was simply failing. My mitral valve was operating more like a doggy door than a one-way valve, and was leaking almost 100%. To compensate for the loss of blood flow, my body naturally doubled the amount of blood that was pushed through my heart; this in turn was putting an immense amount of fluid pressure on my lungs, making it difficult to breathe.

After watching the results from my blood draws over those past couple of weeks, Dr. Bolling and his nurses convened and agreed that it'd be best to move the surgery date up to October 20. That was a more manageable timeframe.

Each week leading up to the surgery, I tried to enjoy every moment to the fullest, knowing life was soon to look different. I was on a high dose of diuretics, which helped me pass the fluids my body was holding; but that meant I had a hard time leaving the house, not knowing how I would feel and if a bathroom would be close by. Mazy used to be scared of public restrooms, but every time we ran errands, I'd have to stop at least twice. She quickly got used to loud public restroom toilets. In the end, she even knew what the Koala baby changing stations were and had to "change" her doll's diaper on them when we made our pit stops. Sadly, it was our new normal.

As the surgery date drew closer and closer, I had an assortment of tests to get a better picture of my heart so that Dr. Bolling would know exactly what he was facing the day of my surgery. Also, not only was I preparing my body for surgery, but we had a few unfinished house projects that we wanted to complete, since I'd be out of commission for a while. I am thankful we had something to keep us busy because otherwise, time would've dragged and I would've started thinking about the surgery too much. Having too much time to think is not always a good thing!

CHAPTER 22

Open Heart Surgery #2

My surgery was scheduled to be the second surgery of the day, but I still had to be at the hospital by 8:00 a.m.; so we decided to leave the night before and stay at the small hotel within the hospital.

On our drive to Ann Arbor, my phone rang; it was the University of Michigan calling. I started to panic as the nurse explained that the ICU floors were full and they had to bump some surgeries back. I started to sweat profusely as my heart began to race. You've got to be kidding me! They had warned me when they scheduled the surgery that sometimes surgeries get bumped for emergencies and so forth. We already had Mazy off to Grandma and Grandpa's and we were already 45 minutes into the 2 ½ hour drive. I had prepared my mind, emotions, and spiritual heart in every way possible, and now the night before my surgery, was I going to have to reschedule?

The nurse went on to say that Dr. Bolling had reviewed the cases and decided what took priority. She continued telling me that when he looked at mine, he recognized that I was a young mom who needed to get fixed now, so my case took precedence and was bumped up to the first case on Friday. I immediately started to cry. I was certain the nurse had been calling to tell me they had bumped my surgery, but instead, she was calling to tell me the surgeon cared enough about our life's situation to still do my surgery on the scheduled day. Needless to say, I had a few drops of sweat to wipe after that phone call!

One thing I wanted to do before my surgery was to Skype with our best friends, Matt and Brianna from Minnesota, who I spoke earlier about. They are the type of friends you can have a spiritual conversation with one minute and be joking about something the next. We met them about six months after we moved to Minnesota and quickly became life-long friends. That night, sitting on the hotel bed with the laptop balanced on our legs, staring at the pixilated image of our friends, we talked about how the surgery was supposed to go and any fears we had. Of course, as usual, there were a few sarcastic comments thrown in by Matt and Dan just to keep things light. We talked for what seemed like hours, and before we knew it, we had to get up in a few hours for my surgery. So off to bed it was, to attempt to get a little sleep.

The alarm went off at 4:45 a.m., ready to rock and roll. But before we walked out the door, we had to have the same dreaded conversation we had before I went into labor with Mazy. What if I didn't make it? As we both cried, Dan reminded me of our desires: I would take care of our two babies in Heaven and he would take care of Mazy. I had also told Matt and Brianna the night before, to make sure Dan got remarried because Mazy needed a mommy, if I couldn't be there. After that tearful conversation, we sat on the edge of the bed and read through Psalm 121; the same Psalm that was read to me before my first open heart surgery when I was 17. We prayed and then it was game time; now or never.

While I was getting prepped, I realized I didn't exactly fit in with the rest of the people getting ready that morning. I was the youngest by about 30 years, and I don't think the nurses were accustomed to someone my age either. Therefore, I took that time to joke around and have some fun with them. It wasn't my first rodeo, so each time they apologized for not being able to get an IV in, I told them eh, it's nothing. Going into this surgery, I really wanted to have a positive attitude. When I had first met with Dr. Bolling, he felt I would recover well and go on to live a normal life, so I was excited to get on with that normal life.

In fact, during that first meeting with Dr. Bolling, he said if he could, he'd take me by the neck and do my surgery right at that moment. He had a daughter about my age and knew the toll it was taking on my life. He was confident that after my surgery, I could go on to have ten more kids and run marathons if I wanted to. I can't say those were my goals, but hey, I would take a normal life!

186

Dan and I did a fist bump, said our goodbyes, and off I went. After the nurses wheeled me back into the operating room, the anesthesiologist put a mask over my nose and mouth, and told me to breathe deeply. He started to count down and all I could think about was how good God had been to me. Whatever happened was His will, not mine. And off to sleep I went.

The surgery was only 2 ½ hours, instead of the three to four hours they expected it to be. By 11:00 a.m., Dan was meeting with Dr. Bolling to hear how the surgery went. Everything went just as planned - a newly repaired, reconstructed, and working mitral valve with zero leakage!

I was put in the ICU, which is routine after open heart surgery, had a ventilator, and was hooked up to more machines than one ever needs to see. And thus began a recovery unlike any other.

As I laid there lifeless, yet quite disturbed by my vent, I sent a signal to Dan by tapping my leg twice, to let him know I was throwing in the towel. Breathing on my own with a breathing tube, was excruciating and exhausting. I honestly felt I couldn't go any further, but I had to. I had to keep fighting. The nurses had to tie my arms down as I relentlessly tried to pull the tube out. Sound familiar from my first surgery?

Apparently I was going to set the floor record for getting my ventilator out the fastest (there's a competition between the nurses, obviously within the parameters of health safety), but the x-ray people were late, so I had to hang on a bit longer. Once the vent was removed, there was freedom for breathing on my own.

The next few days were more challenging than I could've ever imagined. They were not only a test of pain tolerance, but a test of my faith. For some reason, going into this surgery, I felt confident that I could conquer it with ease. Ha! I was proved wrong and my pride was taken down a notch. When the incision was made from my right shoulder blade all the way to under my arm, the doctors and nurses believed some nerves were severed, causing severe nerve damage, which was triggering the immense pain I was feeling. They compared the feeling to being electrocuted on the nerves in your arm, with some maniac cranking up the voltage every few seconds. I would agree with that description wholeheartedly. It was pain that caused me to double over, start to pass out, and even bite a pillow, trying to release the intensity in any way I could. This is completely unlike me and I'd like to say I handled it like a champ, but I didn't.

The doctors and nurses were doing everything they could to help ease the pain. It was deflating to hear the nurse, while holding my hand tell me, "Kristin, we have done everything we can right now," as the episodes continued. They gave me the highest dose of morphine they could, while my body would shake with the rush of adrenaline from the pain. About 15 minutes into each episode and almost passing out, the pain would subside. I would fall asleep for about one or two hours afterward, as my body recovered. The medical team wasn't sure why the pain was so severe, but they believed it would eventually subside. They were right - by Sunday night, I had my last episode.

Not only did I have extreme nerve pain, but I also had severe back pain where my 8-inch incision was sewn up. At the time I was unaware of what the cause of my back pain was, but I later learned that a notch was taken from one of my ribs, so the surgeon could have easier access to my heart. A broken rib sure is no joke, especially since I had to lay on it 24/7.

Thankfully I was in the ICU, so I had the one-on-one attention my pain demanded. I also had an amazing nurse in Cassandra, who cared for me like I was her friend. When your only interaction with the outside world is with the few people that visit and the other patients you see on small walks around the ICU floor, having an outside "friend" to talk to, is comforting.

My health was starting to improve, so two days after surgery I was scheduled to be moved to the stepdown unit. Looking out the window of my hospital room, I could see it was a beautiful day, and on a whim Cassandra asked if I wanted to go outside. It was supposed to be the last nice day before the weather turned cold, and since the nurses in the stepdown unit are spread a little thin, it'd be the perfect opportunity to get some fresh air and feel the warm sun on my face. I quickly learned that being able to go outside was quite the ordeal. I had to get disconnected from the machines and monitors I was currently tethered to, and then get reconnected to portable monitors. We also had to bring along a large plastic box with the words "arrest box" printed in bold letters across the front. I'm not really sure what was in the box, but the word "arrest" has never meant something good.

When we arrived in the courtyard, I couldn't stop smiling. Seeing a few people walking around, taking in a deep breath of air that was different from the sterilized hospital air, and turning my mind off my current situation, was incredibly refreshing.

After my rejuvenating time outside, I was moved to the stepdown unit. This is where the patient becomes more independent and it's the final step before being discharged. I no longer had as many IVs, or a catheter, but still had chest tubes sticking out the side of my abdomen. By Monday night though, I had turned a corner. Dan's brother was visiting at the time, and he noticed I really perked up just in the few hours he was there. I could perhaps have gone home on Tuesday, but I just had my chest tubes removed and wanted one more good day. I wanted to be confident in going home so I could recover well.

One of the most important parts of recovering from open heart surgery is getting up and moving, by walking. Staying active prevents blood clots, encourages blood movement, and gets the heart pumping (all within moderation and within boundaries set by the surgeon). In fact, within 24 hours after surgery, I was up and walking. Those first few steps were difficult, tiring, and excruciating at times, but it's proven that the more active you are after surgery, the quicker you will recover. With that said, anytime I got the chance to walk, I tried. I started with baby steps, but during the last two days, I was able to do laps around the stepdown unit.

By Wednesday, I was discharged. That morning I was given a high dose of diuretics and passed six pounds of fluid in two hours. Losing that much fluid weight so quickly made it easier to breathe, but at the same time, it wiped me out, much like after having Mazy. My body was tired and I slept for the next two hours. After resting that morning, I was feeling good and was confident that I'd do just fine recovering at home. It was surreal climbing out of my hospital bed all on my own and walking out to the hallway where a wheelchair waited for me.

That place had become our home for six days and it felt like so much had happened. We were excited to get home and see Mazy, but at the same time, we were a little sad to be leaving everything that had become familiar. As Dan wheeled me down the hallways and connecting corridors, we saw my surgeon in the atrium eating lunch; I knew I needed a picture with him. When I asked if he would take a picture with me, he said of course, but not while I was sitting in a wheelchair! Standing next to the man God used to heal me was humbling.

The 2 ½ hour drive home went surprisingly well, especially since Dan tried as hard as he could to avoid every bump and pothole.; granted it helped that I slept for almost two hours of it. Mazy was still with Dan's parents and though we missed her incredibly, we thought it'd be best to wait a day and get readjusted to life at home before they brought her into the mix of things. By Thursday morning, we were nipping at the bit to see her! When Dan's parents pulled up to our house that morning, Mazy looked out the window and said, "It's my house!" She was so excited to be home, but as she walked in the door, she realized something was different. She was timid around me at first and didn't really know what to do. I wanted to bend down, scoop her up in my arms and just give her the biggest hug, but I couldn't. Slowly she warmed up to me and realized she could climb up on the couch next to me to snuggle on the left side, opposite of where my incision was. What a blessing that was to be able to snuggle up with her again and look into those bright blue eyes of hers. Now our family was whole again and I could begin my recovery journey at home.

CHAPTER 23

A Turn for the Worst

The first few days at home went so well. I was up and moving, taking small walks, wanting visitors, and sleeping okay. One of the things that I kept telling Mazy was that after I got back from the "doctor," I could take her down to the park. So on Sunday, when I was feeling pretty good, we made the short two-block walk to the park. I couldn't pull her in a wagon, so Dan came along to assist. The air was cold, and it hurt to breathe, but it felt so good to be outside again. I made it to the park just fine, but on the walk back, I got quite tired and had to stop halfway. Was I too weak? Was I pushing too hard? I didn't think so, but I figured that was the farthest I had walked since surgery, so in my mind it made sense.

By nighttime, I became extremely tired. Dan had to leave for youth group, but thankfully I had a friend over who could help get Mazy ready for bed while I rested. It was just a bad day, right? I was told to expect them. The next day, I still felt tired and a little short of breath, but enjoyed a visit from my cousin in the morning and took a nap in the afternoon. By then though, I felt like I was getting the flu because I was feeling achy and winded. The visiting nurse stopped by for her routine appointment and we both thought I was maybe coming down with something, so she suggested to just take it easy for a while. By nighttime, I should've known something else was wrong.

I went to bed the same time Mazy did, which was at 8:30. I woke up numerous times that night, feeling nauseous. I was soaking wet from sweat, and just couldn't get comfortable in any position except upright. Finally morning came and by 7:30 I made it to the kitchen chair, but could only lay my head on my arms. I was able to get my pills down and a few saltines, but it was a struggle. I took my vitals and something was clearly not right. My oxygen was about 89% and my weight was up at least five pounds. What was happening?

Slowly I got up and staggered back to bed. Meanwhile, Dan was getting Mazy ready for the morning, and also tried getting himself ready for work. While he was in the shower, Mazy came into our room and could tell something was wrong. She brought me her cherished blanket and every stuffed animal she could fit into her arms. She dragged her step stool to the edge of the bed, wiggled her way up, and began to wipe my forehead with a rag. Was it that obvious that something was wrong that a two-year-old could even tell?

Our friend Val, who is a nurse, was going to stay with me that day so Dan could work. Shortly after she arrived and Dan left, the visiting nurse program called because my vitals raised a red flag. I couldn't even talk on the phone because I was so short of breath. They suggested sending a nurse out to see me, but as Val spoke with them on the phone, it became apparent that I needed to go to the emergency room right away.

I was still in my robe, but at that point, I didn't even care, so Val helped me get some socks, pants, and a coat on. She asked if she should call for an ambulance, but I was confident I could get to the car; or so I thought. I grabbed my wallet and cell phone, and tried to walk out the door, but couldn't do it on my own. I was so weak. My legs were shaking uncontrollably, so Val helped me down the steps and into the car. I don't remember much of that short ride, except thinking that something was happening and it wasn't good.

It was no mistake that God had purposefully scheduled Val to stay with me that day. Little did we both know that she was exactly what I needed. A medical professional who knew what to do in a situation like this. Someone who knew that I wasn't okay, but didn't panic. Someone who knew what was best for me.

When we got to the hospital's ER, Val didn't even park the car, but drove right up to the door, helped me get into a wheelchair, and pushed me through the sliding doors into the emergency room. She explained to the intake receptionist that I recently had open heart surgery, was short of breath, and lethargic. Before I even realized what was going on, within seconds of Val saying, "Open heart surgery, short of breath, and lethargic," a nurse grabbed me and wheeled me into a monitoring room.

Multiple people started to come into the room, as I struggled to get a hospital gown on and simply breathe. Thankfully Val, who had worked in that exact ER department, was able to explain to the nurses and doctor my symptoms. The doctor couldn't pinpoint exactly what was wrong, so they ordered a CT scan. As they slid me into the machine, I was told to put my arms above my head. Didn't they know I just had open heart surgery and didn't have the range of motion to do that? Somehow, I did it, but from there, things went blurry as I started to lose consciousness. The next thing I knew, the room flooded with medical staff shouting to get me out and sit me upright. My vitals had gone crazy, and as they pulled me out and put me vertical, things started to become clear and I could breathe a little easier. It was a scary moment, but a telling moment at that.

After receiving some IV fluids, Zofran (an anti-nausea med), and oxygen, I was feeling much better. I suppose that was relative at the time, but at least I was able to have a conversation. By this time, Dan and my mom had arrived. The doctor came in and though I should've seen this coming, it still came as a bit of a shock. He looked at them and said, "Really, we need to get her back to the University of Michigan, and we have Aero Med inbound to take her there."

I wasn't sure I had heard him correctly, so I replayed those words in my head again. And again. I looked at Dan and my mom as they intently listened to what that meant. At the time, there was question that maybe my gall bladder was causing issues, since I had such an intense pain on the right side by my rib cage. My blood tests showed an incredible amount of fluid built up, but it was unclear where the fluid was. At that point, we weren't sure if my heart was okay, but because I had just had a surgery to repair my valve, it seemed odd that I was retaining so much fluid in my body. So they were thinking it was maybe an infection, along with pneumonia.

Meanwhile, what seemed like a few short minutes later (though I am sure it was longer than that), I could hear the rotor blades of a helicopter beating the air as it circled over the hospital, beginning its descent. Was that really for ME? Was I that sick?

It was Halloween, and Dan's mom had made the cutest puppy costume for Mazy. I knew Mazy was looking forward to trick-

or-treating in her costume, so I looked at Dan and said, "Make sure you take Mazy trick-or-treating before you drive to Michigan."

Three people dressed in flight suits came walking into the cramped exam room, and realized they were indeed here for me. I was still shocked that I was sick enough to have to be flown back to the University of Michigan. Only people in serious need of medical attention were flown on Aero Med.

I was strapped in the gurney and wrapped up with blankets as nurses came from around their stations in the ER to wish me well. Dan and my mom walked with me out to the helicopter, as they slid me in the back. The nurses explained everything that was going to happen and told me to tell them anytime I felt pain, since their goal was to keep me as comfortable as possible. How we all fit in there I'm not sure! The back of the helicopter was jammed full of every monitor and medical device that a modern emergency room would have, plus two folding jump seats for the flight nurses. A nurse put a headset on me so I could tell them if I needed anything, as they assumed their designated places.

The blades started up and within seconds, we were in the air for the 45-minute flight to Michigan. I could not make sense of it all. What's wrong with me? What were the doctors at Michigan going to do that the doctors at my local hospital couldn't?

Many have asked what it was like to ride in a helicopter. I would love to say it was the most awesome ride of my life, but honestly, I probably slept through half of it. I wanted to just get there because I felt so sick, was uncomfortable, and wanted to wish it all away. I did look outside at the green trees starting to turn yellow, and the nurses did take the time to point out the Big House to me. I am a die-hard Michigan football fan, so if there was any highlight, it was definitely that.

As a kid, and even now as an adult, anytime I saw Aero Med my heart always sank. To think that someone was that injured or that sick that a helicopter was the best route, was always heart-breaking to think about. Now to think that was me in there was something I didn't fully comprehend or deal with until later.

After getting wheeled into the ER at the University of Michigan, it felt like it was straight out of the movies. I wasn't even in a room yet when people started popping out from all over, surrounding my bed. I was hooked up to multiple machines as both doctors and nurses asked about my symptoms. Soon after arriving, they did an ECHO. After attempting to get one image, the technician asked me to do a quick sniff through my nose, but I had no breath to do so. The technician insisted that I try again because they needed to get a better image. I tried one more time and sure enough, my vitals went awry. Someone stepped in and said, "She CAN'T DO IT." Thank you to whoever that was!

After getting some more pain meds, I was able to rest a bit, and waited to see what was next. I still didn't know what was wrong. Was it just my gall bladder? If so, just take it out! It would be another surgery, but bring it on. I was transferred to an ER ICU room, as multiple doctors came in and out, trying to figure out what was wrong. By this time, the cardiac team was also involved, which had me a bit worried.

After seeing the results of my blood tests, doctors were certain I had a gall bladder infection because it was severely inflamed. The goal was to either take it out the next day or just drain it for four to six weeks and then remove it after I was more stable. In reality though, the treatment plan was changing by the hour.

The day after my arrival, I had a handful of more tests and by the afternoon, my cardiac surgeon was able to stop by. I was thrilled to see a familiar face, so I excitedly welcomed him with a smile. It was such a chaotic time that seeing someone who knew my history was comforting.

Of course he had to give me grief for being back, though I certainly wasn't ready for the news he was about to give me. He took a listen to my heart for literally two seconds. No exaggeration. In a frustrated voice he said, "That's not the same heart I heard last Wednesday when you left here." At that point, I wasn't fully convinced something was wrong with my heart, but thought it was just my gall bladder.

Then he broke the news to me that would change my life. Not necessarily for the good at the time, but in the end, change my spiritual heart for the good. You see, when God puts trials and tests in front of us, for the present time, they may seem burdensome, but in the end, God turns them for good. Because that is just how our great and good God works, like I said before.

His words are still so vividly etched in my mind: "I don't think your mitral valve is functioning at all. That means you will need to have another open heart surgery. The problem is I am supposed to leave for Vietnam tomorrow morning, so my colleague, Dr. Pagani, is going to perform the surgery, and he is someone I would have operate on me."

Even though he wasn't certain, he believed that the heart valve had become infected from the bile that was built up in the gall bladder, causing it to leak. Therefore, the mitral valve repair didn't hold and he'd have to go back in and repair it, if not replace the valve.

Wait, another open heart surgery? I just had one 12 days ago. Wasn't there another way? Another way to fix the problem? I thought it was a perfect fix! When I was discharged, my valve was functioning perfectly. What happened?

Did the surgeon also say a possible *replacement*? What we were so thankful for before was that I did not need a replacement. I didn't want to revisit the issue of whether to have a tissue or mechanical valve. I was only 33.

It was all so surreal. There was no way that this was happening.

I know my surgeon struggled to tell me that news and as soon as he walked out, I just wept. How? Why? I was supposed to be on the road to a normal life after my first surgery. I was supposed to be living a life that led to marathons if I wanted to (even though that wasn't a goal of mine). I was supposed to be "normal." My heart issues were supposed to be behind me so that I could be the mom I wanted to be for Mazy, and the healthy mom she needed. I just wanted to be a mom who could walk with her daughter to the park.

They hoped to be able to do the second surgery soon, but I wasn't stable enough, so they'd have to wait a few days. Two open heart surgeries in a little over two weeks? No way. I couldn't even wrap my head around it, let alone believe that I could do it. I had three broken ribs (which we didn't know about at the time), an 8-inch scar from under my armpit around to the back of my shoulder blade that was still healing, and two chest tube scars. My heart was just stopped and now they would have to stop it again; would it start up again after another surgery?

After I gathered myself, I called my mom. How could the news that I was telling her actually be true? It was so hard to speak the words "another open heart surgery." As always though, I think I just needed to hear my mom's voice because after I spoke with her, it seemed like everything was going to be okay. Moms have a way of doing that, don't they?

Late Wednesday afternoon, I was moved up to the cardiac ICU. It was a strange and surreal feeling being back on the floor that I was on two weeks prior. In an odd way, it felt kind of like a homecoming. When we left after my first surgery, we thought we'd never see some of the nurses or doctors ever again. Here I was though, getting wheeled down the hallway on a gurney. Different nurses would look at us and you could see the wheels turning in their heads as they finally recognized us from our previous stay. We heard lots of comments along the lines of, "Hey, good to see you again, just wish it was under different circumstances."

Then we ran into my nurse Cassandra, who I had the entire time I was in the ICU for the first go around. She looked at us as her jaw dropped and exclaimed, "What are you doing back here?" The thing was, we didn't really know the answer yet. We knew all the symptoms I was feeling, we knew my mitral valve was failing, but we really didn't know the exact reason why. All we knew was that I needed another open heart surgery and possibly gall bladder surgery as well.

I was told that the cardiac doctor was extremely worried and had everyone who was available working on my case, to try and determine what was wrong. It was obvious the valve wasn't functioning, but why? Why was the gall bladder acting up? The doctor was doing lots of research, trying to figure out what my symptoms meant; a strange case that was befuddling them and had him scared. I am thankful they didn't tell me that at the time, but it just goes to show how serious the situation was.

Wednesday night, still thinking I had a gall bladder infection, the doctors ordered what is called a HIDA (hepatobiliary) scan. A dye is injected into the body that flows through the gall bladder, and eventually into the small intestines. A large scanner is then placed over the torso that sends real time images back to a computer, much like an ultrasound does. The purpose of the test was to see how well the gall bladder was functioning. Seemed like a simple test, but oh was I wrong.

Ever since I had arrived back at Michigan, I wasn't allowed to eat. Everyone thought I was going to be rushed into some type of surgery at any moment, so all I was allowed to have were ice chips. When the dye for the test was injected, since I had an empty stomach, it made me feel incredibly nauseous and cramp up. To make matters worse, I had to lie flat on my back. The fluid building up in my chest cavity was putting pressure on my lungs, making it difficult to get a full breath of air, and was also putting pressure on my three broken ribs. All of this made for excruciating pain. So for one hour, I doubled over in pain, squeezing Dan's hand and turning it white, making the machines that recorded my vitals go berserk.

The whole time Dan just kept telling me, "You can do this, take it in 10-minute increments. You can do anything for 10 minutes. When that 10 minutes is up, focus on the next 10 minutes." Then it turned into 5 minutes because 10 minutes was too long. After experiencing the most debilitating pain I had ever felt and again almost passing out, the nurse finally caved. She was getting extremely frustrated with the technician because my vitals were skyrocketing. The problem was that I couldn't take any pain meds because it would interfere with the test. Finally, with 18 minutes left, she firmly said I had to get something in me or the technician would have to stop the test. Within minutes after receiving some medication, I finally took a deep breath and exhaled with somewhat ease. My body finally stopped shaking from the pain and my vitals regulated.

Meanwhile, the cardiac doctor on shift that night came in saying that after researching my symptoms, talking with other medical professionals for the last four hours, and looking at the results of the gall bladder tests thus far, he didn't think it was the gall bladder. He felt there was some other reason for the fluid buildup.

Sure enough, the tests confirmed there were no gall bladder issues; it was functioning just fine. The mitral valve had not failed due to an infection of my gall bladder. He felt that for some reason the valve repair had failed on its own, and the excess fluid was putting pressure on my heart, lungs, and other organs (including the gall bladder), causing signs and symptoms of a gall bladder infection. Therefore, no gall bladder surgery was needed. That was one positive step in the right direction! Up until that point, I was looking at TWO more surgeries – my gall bladder and another open heart surgery. So, when I say a positive step, that news brought much relief.

On Thursday, November 2, after getting a tube called a swan inserted into my neck, with no sedation (I would NOT recommend that). I then had a TEE (transesophageal echocardiogram), which they weren't going to sedate me for, due to my instability, but I begged them. Not another procedure without sedation! My nurse knew what happened with my last test (the HIDA scan) and how my vitals went crazy, and after weighing the risks, the doctor realized that my body couldn't take any more pain. Call it what it was – post-traumatic stress disorder (PTSD). Mentally I just couldn't take anymore.

I remember expressing to Dan how I just couldn't handle any more pain. I couldn't keep going. I couldn't do one more test. I even told the doctor I couldn't do it and that is so unlike me. Not that I was chickening out, but all the tests I had took a toll on me. I have learned the neck is a sensitive area and after getting a ¼-inch tube inserted into it, fully awake, is no walk in the park. Usually those are inserted during a surgery; but I was under different circumstances. Thankfully the nurse vouched for me and they ended up sedating me for the TEE.

Sure enough, the TEE proved what we were afraid of – that the valve repair was toast. Before my valve was repaired, my heart had increased the amount of blood that it was pushing through to compensate for the regurgitation in the failed valve. We knew that it'd take a few months for my heart to re-regulate the amount of blood that it was pushing through. However, the tissue around my valve had become so hardened and calcified over the years, and when the excess blood began to build up behind the repaired valve, it created so much pressure that it ripped through the sutures that held my valve together. I can only imagine what was going on in my body when that happened.

It wasn't that my surgeon did anything wrong. In fact, he performed a perfect surgery and my valve was working perfectly for what we believed was at least nine days. Dr. Bolling is one of only three cardiac surgeons in the United States who performs well over 100 mitral valve repairs in a year, and has a success rate that exceeds 99%.[13] So for the repair of my mitral valve to fail was quite rare. We had hoped that after the repair that I would live a life as if I never had a heart problem to begin with, but God had a different plan. And I had to trust that it would be good and for the good.

I was scheduled to have another open heart surgery either that weekend or on Monday. The reason the day was unknown was because my body and heart still weren't stable enough at that point. So, we'd have to wait. Since Dr. Bolling, my first surgeon was gone,

Dr. Pagani would for sure be performing this surgery. Dr. Pagani specializes in heart transplants, but is also well known for doing second surgeries/repeats. I would've loved for Dr. Bolling to do the surgery, but we were very confident in Dr. Pagani's skills. A surgeon who was also known for re-dos? Only God. And only His grace. In fact, Dr. Pagani was willing to come in at any hour to do my surgery, knowing the sensitivity of the situation. Also, this time they'd have to saw through my sternum in the same fashion as the surgeons did for my very first open heart surgery when I was 17. Going through my side, where I already had a fresh scar, wasn't an option.

Also, my original valve was for sure damaged beyond repair, so we had to choose whether I wanted to go with a mechanical or a tissue valve. It was a decision I dreaded making, but God was right there with us. He sent just the right people to encourage and help us make that decision. Nurses, cardiac fellows, and doctors, all took the time to sit down with us and give us their thoughts. To this day, we believe they were sent by God to give us that tangible peace that we so desperately needed. Our minds and emotions were so drained; God knew we needed them to help make a logical and right decision.

Though a mechanical valve would last the rest of my life, we weren't excited about the side effects of me being on a blood thinner the rest of my life. A tissue valve would last only about 10 to 15 years, but studies are starting to show they could last longer. We were also encouraged by the advancement in medical technology with valve replacement and were hopeful that when the tissue valve did need to be replaced, the technology would be in place to do a less invasive procedure. So after praying about the options, talking with others, and discussing what we thought would be best, Dan and I decided that a tissue valve was the best option.

Despite how devastated we were that this was all happening, we had this supernatural peace within us. We already had been given many opportunities to share about our faith. All along, we prayed that whatever it took for God's name to be furthered, then that's what we wanted. It was a nerve-wracking prayer to pray because little did we know that it'd lead to me having another open heart surgery. Was I really ready to stand up to the test? We sure cried. We sure wondered why. Though we knew if God called us to this, He would then equip us.

God sees. God knows. God hears. That is a saying that my dear friend Brenda has reminded me of time and time again. Six words, once again, filled with such promise, love, and comfort. Six words we were hanging onto by a thread when we thought things couldn't get worse.

It was about 11:00 p.m. on Thursday, November 2, and I had just blown an arterial line (catheter placed into an artery). The nurse was busy performing an ultrasound to find a good artery, when two PAs walked in. I quickly said, "Good news, right?" Their somber faces should've been a clue.

"No Kristin, this is not good news."

My heart sank even further down, if that was even possible. I couldn't take one more blow. I couldn't take one more test. Please tell me it was just something minor.

A recent test had proven that since my mitral valve was completely shot, my heart wasn't pumping blood to my vital organs like my kidneys and liver, which could end up causing permanent damage, if not taken care of in the next few hours. Those words flew right by my ears. It was too surreal. I thought my situation was already critical. I couldn't help but ask God, why?

They were going to increase a medication in hopes of seeing improvement, but for the past six hours, there was no improvement. For the record, I was unaware I was even on a medication to help with my organ function. If in the next two hours the numbers didn't rise, they were going to have to open my chest, insert a bypass pump around the valve called an AVAD, and then leave me sedated with my chest cavity open until my heart stabilized. Then they could perform the second open heart surgery.

I didn't know how to ask this question because I never had to and never imagined it being me – but I finally got the words out: "Is this a life and death situation?" They said no, but if something wasn't done, then yes, it would turn into that. In my mind, anytime someone needed to be sedated heavily so that a machine could be inserted into their body to keep it running, it felt like a life-threatening situation. I knew if it had to be done, I needed to succumb to the realities of the situation. The realities that I was very sick and that this could end up taking my life if something wasn't done, was shocking.

You just never imagine it being YOU. You never imagine having that conversation with someone. The PAs were so gracious and willing to answer any and every question I had.

They suggested I call Dan immediately. It was then that I realized it truly was very serious. How was I going to tell Dan? I asked the PAs if they would be willing to talk to Dan instead after he came. It was already a long night, so Dan had just headed to bed when I called him. I immediately cut to the chase and said he needed to come to my room immediately because something happened. Thankfully he was just at the Med Inn, which was the hotel on the hospital campus, so he was there within minutes. He arrived and I told him to go find James, the nurse practitioner, who we had been working with. After Dan came back to my room, we just wept. We finally broke. How much more, God? How much more could we take?

Dan knew that it'd be hard to sit in my ICU room while I laid there sedated with my chest cavity still open, if it came to that. How was he to look at his wife, lifeless, for days? I told him that if this ended up happening, to please go home for the next few days, until my surgery. I wouldn't know the difference and he needed to protect his mind and heart. I knew he loved me, but I didn't want him to see me that way.

Dan texted a few of our Minnesota friends who he knew would still be up (thanks to the one-hour time difference), along with a few Michigan friends, explaining the quick turn of events, asking them to pray. Tears fell non-stop, as Dan and I fervently prayed for God to take this burden from us and heal my heart.

Pastor Steve, our pastor from our church back in Minnesota, had told us to read Psalm 77:1-15 from the Message. Talk about getting hit right between the eyes. These verses were an extension of our heart and gave us immense comfort:

Psalm 77:1-15 from The Message (MSG)
I yell out to my God, I yell with all my might,
  I yell at the top of my lungs. He listens.
I found myself in trouble and went looking for my Lord;
  my life was an open wound that wouldn't heal.
When friends said, "Everything will turn out all right,"
  I didn't believe a word they said.
I remember God — and shake my head.
  I bow my head — then wring my hands.
I'm awake all night — not a wink of sleep;
  I can't even say what's bothering me.
I go over the days one by one,

I ponder the years gone by.
I strum my lute all through the night,
  wondering how to get my life together.
Will the Lord walk off and leave us for good?
  Will he never smile again?
Is his love worn threadbare?
  Has his salvation promise burned out?
Has God forgotten his manners?
  Has he angrily stalked off and left us?
"Just my luck," I said. "The High God goes out of
  business just the moment I need him."
Once again I'll go over what God has done,
  lay out on the table the ancient wonders;
I'll ponder all the things you've accomplished,
  and give a long, loving look at your acts.
O God! Your way is holy!
  No god is great like God!
You're the God who makes things happen;
  you showed everyone what you can do —
You pulled your people out of the worst kind of trouble,
  rescued the children of Jacob and Joseph.

The meds started working in the first half hour which got our hopes up, but then slowed down after that. We knew that the lower numbers from the tests meant they'd have to go ahead with the procedure to insert this bypass pump. It seemed inevitable. Within hours, I'd be going under the knife and sawed open to have this bypass pump put in. I kept looking at Dan, thinking just a few more hours and our lives would, once again, never be the same.

After those two hours went by, we thought every footstep in the hallway was the doctor coming in to prep me for surgery.

Though after the initial shock of the possibility, we were still filled with a peace that surpasses all understanding. I got to the point where I was ready to do whatever it took for me to get better.

Three long hours later, James finally came in and said that after talking with the surgeon on the phone, they were comfortable with where things were and decided not to open me up. However, they would revisit that option in the morning; though by this time, it was already into the wee hours of the morning. As we spoke with him, Dan faithfully told him, "We believe in a sovereign God who is in control, and you guys do what you need to do."

Dan gave me a quick kiss and headed back to his room to get a few hours of sleep. We both slept incredibly well those next few hours, knowing that time of rest was such a gift!

Early the next morning, so really just a few short hours later, James came in with shocking news: I could finally eat and drink.

WHAT? I went from being hours away from going into surgery to now eating? I hadn't had anything to drink or eat since Tuesday morning. Remember those saltines I tried to eat? That was my last taste of food; and now it was Friday morning. Granted, I could swab my mouth with water and suck on ice chips, but that was it. A swab dipped in water does nothing to satisfy thirst. All it does is make your lips not stick to your gums as much. After not eating or drinking for that long, weakness starts to set in, so being told I could drink water and eat real food, I felt like I won a trip to Disney World. Okay, maybe the Caribbean.

Meanwhile, Dan woke up that morning, quickly got ready, and power walked from his hotel room in the hospital to my room in the cardiac ICU, not knowing what condition he would find me in. He walked in, saw me sitting up in bed eating breakfast, and noticed it was solid food. Instantly, he realized that solid food meant there was no surgery or bypass pump planned in the near future.

209

Dan knelt by my bedside and wept. We just wept. So many emotions built up over the past few hours and days. We FINALLY reached the point where things were looking up.

The days leading up to the next open heart surgery definitely weren't always easy, but we made it. I remember telling Dan that I just wanted a few good days to get somewhat healthy, so that I could go into my second surgery with some strength. Some sort of will power, since I felt I had lost all of it. Well, God granted those desires to me and gave me Saturday and Sunday to recuperate and rest.

Saturday night, Dan had the opportunity to go to the Minnesota vs. Michigan football game at the Big House. A former youth group kid of ours from Minnesota, who now lived in Michigan, had an extra ticket and asked Dan if he'd like to go. Dan started asking me and before he finished I said, "GO! You have to GO! I'd be upset if you didn't!" In fact, it'd make me feel good knowing that someone was representing us! During our time in Ann Arbor, we kept saying how cool it would be if we could go to a game. Well of course that always meant Dan, since I was in no condition to go to a football game. He needed to get out of the hospital and have some fun. And Michigan won, in case you were wondering. Meanwhile, I was able to rest and relax, which surprisingly is hard to do in the ICU due to all the tests and tubes, but needless to say, it was a much needed "good" night for the both of us.

CHAPTER 24

Open Heart Surgery #3

Monday, surgery day, finally came. The surgery was scheduled for 7:00 a.m., so Dan came to my room at around 5:30 to visit one last time. We spent the waiting period praying, listening to worship music, replaying the song, *"King of My Heart"* by Bethel Music. What peace that song brought! God surely was the King of my heart, in more ways than one.

As I was being wheeled into the operating room, I asked how long the surgery would be. The nurse said about six to eight hours; then he added that the surgery was a little more risky this time around. Was I again entering a room where I would have to think about this being my last moments? Laying on that table, I truly couldn't believe this all was happening again, yet it all felt so normal. Everything was the same. Everything was familiar. But this time, my body didn't want to go under. I kept wishing it would just succumb to the anesthesia they were giving me, but it was difficult to take deep breaths through the mask over my face. The longer it took, the more I started to panic; but finally, my body gave in.

From what I was told, the surgery went very well, and there were no complications. They ended up replacing my mitral valve with a tissue valve that was made from tissue in a cow's valve. It seemed only fitting for the daughter of a dairy farmer to get a new valve made from cow parts. Dr. Pagani was able to put a rather large valve in so that someday, when it needs to be replaced, they can actually put a new valve inside of the old valve. During the surgery, Dr. Pagani also decided to repair my tricuspid valve, since that was also leaking. I guess he figured he might as well do it while he was in there.

About six hours later, Dan and his parents were finally able to come back to the cardiac ICU and see me.

From my previous surgery, Dan knew I didn't come out of sedation well while on a ventilator. As my body starts to become coherent, it starts to work against the vent. It feels like trying to breathe through a straw shoved down your throat, and at times when you are trying to exhale, the vent is trying to push air into your lungs. You can't swallow either, so you are constantly gagging on saliva and mucus stuck in your throat.

Dan warned the nurse ahead of time so she would be prepared. In my semi-conscious state, I usually tried to pull the vent out on my own, so Dan along with his mom, had to hold my arms down the entire time, once again. My nurse was doing everything to hurry along the process and get the vent out as soon as it was safe to do so. My oxygen levels were looking good, and I was about 20

212

minutes away from getting the vent tube out of my throat when a PA came in concerned that I wasn't on any pain medication after just coming out of open heart surgery. So the PA immediately ordered a cocktail of pain meds, which the nurse administered. The downside of pain medications is that it makes the heart rate drop as well as the oxygen levels, which both needed to reach a certain level before the vent could be removed. Instantly I went from being 20 minutes away from having the vent taken out, to who knows when.

For the next three hours, I tried to clear my throat while trying to breathe with this foreign object in my mouth. I started hitting the top of the bed with my hand, and Dan's mom looked at him with eyes that asked, "Is this normal?" To which Dan replied, "She's trying to tap out." I was done with this vent; I couldn't take it anymore and I was giving up.

It's funny how the thing that was supposed to help me breathe actually made it harder to do so. When the body starts to fight the vent, a distinct horn starts honking. In the days that followed while I was still in the ICU, any time Dan heard a patient down the hall start to fight the vent and the horn started honking, he would get on edge.

I started to hyperventilate due to pain, so the nurse gave me more pain meds after she realized I wasn't coming off of it anytime soon. I even wrote messages to Dan and his parents on a note pad, begging them to take it out. At one point, Dan just couldn't take it anymore and stepped out, which I am thankful he did. I can't imagine watching someone go through it myself. It was through their playing of music, singing, and holding of my hands, that I once again, made it through.

Finally, my heart rate and oxygen levels were high enough and the vent could come out. The first thing I said was, "Sorry, guys." I was so sorry that it had taken so long. I know there was nothing to be sorry about, but I was with it enough to know the agony it was causing everyone.

A little while later, Dan and his parents went to get dinner, but when he came back, I was in so much pain. I just laid there in bed moaning. At one point between the moans, I said to Dan, "I sound like a cow." Trying to fight back laughter, Dan said, "Baby, that's because you are part cow now. They put in a cow tissue valve." I didn't really understand what that meant at the time, nor did I find it particularly funny, but now I can understand the humor in his comment.

By the next morning, I was starting to feel better with the pain somewhat under control. The goal for the day was to get up and walk. This seemed to be a lofty goal since I hadn't walked since a week prior. It was a struggle to sit upright, let alone stand up. Somehow with the help of the nurses though, I was able to stand and take my first steps in over 7 days. I couldn't believe I was up and walking! It was slow and it wasn't far, but I was WALKING less than 24 hours after my second surgery.

Two days later, the two tubes circling around in my chest cavity, draining fluid, were taken out. Even though I was making great strides, it was still an up and down battle. Some days I could barely make it out of the room to walk, while other days, if I pushed it, I could do an entire lap around the ICU floor. It was all part of being a cardiac patient.

Thursday, November 9, was a big day. I was moved from the ICU to the stepdown unit, also known as 4C. The day before though, I cried many tears with my parents. I was wrestling with feeling so weak, while others felt I was so strong. I just didn't feel the strength that others saw in me. I couldn't do the things I wanted to do, like something as simple as walking or controlling my pain. It was the night before that move to 4C that my nurse, Xihua, helped me bring my pain levels down to less than a 5 on the pain scale. Her goal that entire night was for me to do nothing, but for her to do everything for me, so I wouldn't waste energy. She wanted my body to have all the energy it could, to heal. It truly transformed how I felt that night and I was finally ready for the move.

You would think I would've been excited to move down to the other floor, but to be quite honest, it was hard to say goodbye to the people we had grown a relationship with on that ICU floor. After being there for my first surgery, and now for the last nine days, it felt like we were saying goodbye to family again.

My journey in the stepdown unit was very up and down. The first few days went well, thanks to a visit from my younger sister and mom. Having family there made time fly and also aided in my emotional stability. By Sunday though, I hit a wall. I teared up about every little thing, felt homesick, wanted to be with my church family, I missed Mazy, and because I was becoming more mentally aware of what was going on, I started to realize what had all just happened. Everything came to a head that day.

Then one particular night, a nurse practitioner came in to see how I was doing. I looked at her and was brutally honest: "It hurts so much." Then she said something that blew me away. "Well of COURSE you are going to hurt! You have four broken bones!" FOUR? At that time, I only knew of my sternum. She then took the time to show Dan and me the x-ray, and I couldn't believe what I saw. I started to tear up because I finally had an explanation as to why I was in so much pain.

Like I said before, with my previous surgery, the surgeon went through my side and cut a notch in one of the ribs (again, at that time, we didn't know this information). Also, a tool is used to spread the ribs apart. In the process, it's not uncommon for ribs to break. Unbeknownst to me, I had two ribs that broke, on top of the notched rib. Remember how much pain I was in with my first surgery? My ribs were just hanging there. Then during my second surgery, when the surgeon went through my sternum and spread my chest cavity wide open, those three ribs that were broken were now displaced again, and moved even more. I'm sure they had told me this at one point, but at that moment, it was news to me. On top of that, my sternum was sawed in half and now held together by internal wires.

I finally didn't feel so guilty and wimpy about asking for my pain meds anytime they were due. All of those tests, when I was first brought back to the hospital, required me to lie flat on my back or side. They were done on three broken ribs that moved right along with me.

Despite the broken bones, one thing I learned as a cardiac patient was that up and down days were normal and expected. If they didn't happen, well, then you weren't really "normal." I found that for me, the healing journey had just seemed so long already, that when any obstacle got in my way, it felt like a mountainous setback. I quickly had to learn that there wasn't much I could do, but just listen to my body and accept the setbacks.

On Tuesday, I was feeling quite well, but wanted just one more good day before heading home, just like with the first surgery. I wanted to go home confident in knowing I wouldn't be back until my post-operation appointment.

By Wednesday, it was time to be discharged after 16 days in the hospital. As Dan wheeled me out, I wasn't sure if I would cry tears of fear or feel a bittersweetness of leaving our home for those past 16 days, but I found myself doing neither. I felt incredible peace, knowing that all those who cared for me during my stay, helped me get to a time such as this. I had peace knowing that God had carried us through the storm, peace knowing that I can do this at home, and peace knowing God's got this and, therefore, so do I.

CHAPTER 25

A Long Road to Recovery

My recovery at home was a bumpy road. During the first four weeks back home, I landed back in the local ER twice and as a result, back at Michigan twice. Each time, I was experiencing weight gain, shortness of breath, loss of appetite, low blood pressures, and fevers. The first visit back to Michigan was only a week after being home, but was cleared to return home that day. At the other visit, they asked that I come in and stay overnight for observation. I couldn't get through one week without some type of setback, which was frustrating and wearing. I started to really wonder if I'd ever get over this hump and if this was what recovery was supposed to look like.

Well, yes it was. I was warned that I'd have good and bad days, though I think my definition of a good and bad day was a bit different. I didn't expect ER and hospital trips.

One thing I wrestled with was unexplainable fevers. They wouldn't spike above 101 degrees, but they made me feel worn out and sometimes ill. Then finally, at the start of the fourth week at home, I finally had my last fever. Looking back, I realized how much they affected my activity level, energy, and mental capacity.

Twice a week, for the first five weeks, a visiting nurse and a physical therapist came to our home. I looked forward to every visit from each of them because so much of what I thought to be "normal" wasn't, thanks to their professional expertise. They helped me grasp that my recovery was a bit unlike others, due to the nature of having two surgeries so close together. They helped me understand that I needed to give myself some grace too. As much as I wanted to be up and about, my body was telling me in every way, that it had a whole lot of healing to do. The simple act of getting up and out of a chair proved to be difficult since I couldn't use my arms. Learning what it meant to take care of myself was more work than I could've ever anticipated. Someone needed to be with me 24/7 if Mazy was at home, since I was unable to lift her or help her with any "mom" tasks.

If it weren't for my mom, I would've been lost. She faithfully came every day to sit with me or take Mazy. She cleaned our home, did our laundry, got our groceries, and made us meals. Her unconditional love, the love of a mom, was exactly what I needed when I couldn't care for myself. She was that emotional support when I couldn't be the mom I wanted to be for Mazy. For me, it tore an already damaged heart into emotional pieces, being unable to care for her.

And I couldn't make sense of those emotional pieces. While in the hospital, I started to experience some pretty intense feelings of fear. I would replay scenarios over and over in my head, starting to question if they were really true. Unfortunately they were, but I found myself getting stuck in those moments. I couldn't exit my mind out of the situations like when I was told I had to be flown back to Michigan. That I'd need another open heart surgery. That I'd possibly need a bypass pump inserted if my stats didn't improve. Moments that led me to fears and eventually tears.

It was during a late night visit from a PA after my second open heart surgery, when I realized something was wrong. She had asked me how I was doing emotionally and I just lost it. I told her I heard a helicopter fly over and I completely froze and cried. I would see certain people and could only associate negative scenarios with them. As I spilled out my fears, she kindly and confidently told me that I was experiencing post-traumatic stress disorder (PTSD).

Even though I knew I had it, it still was a foreign idea to me; though after I arrived home, I couldn't get a grasp on the emotions of what had just occurred. My pastor asked if he could come over to talk (who, if you remember, is a good friend of mine from college). I knew I had a lot to work through, so I accepted. Within minutes of him walking through our door, I was in tears. I held on to so much fear and anxiety from my past, that it was inhibiting me from making any forward progress mentally and emotionally. I feared another open heart surgery. I feared having to go back to Michigan (where I ended up going back twice). I feared being in pain the rest of my life. I feared not getting better. I even feared not giving God the full glory for what He had already done in my life. I feared disappointing Him. I feared that I missed opportunities to talk about God while in the hospital. PTSD got the best of me.

My pastor helped me realize so much about myself during those trying first few weeks at home. Thankfully he knew me and knew how my brain worked. I sure had a hard time letting go of the fear and letting God take control. I had a hard time resting and allowing others to minister to me, instead of having to be the one ministering to others. Really, I had no idea how to give MYSELF grace.

It took a few weeks to learn what rest and grace meant; rest for my body and grace for my soul. The more time I allowed my mind to just rest in Christ, the more those fears started to dissipate. The more I let people into my life, the more physical rest I found, and the more grace I gave myself. I finally became okay in asking for help.

We were shown so much love by our friends and family! People who would pick Mazy up to watch her for a few hours so I could rest. The meals that came so frequently that we started a stockpile in our freezer. The cards sent to encourage us. The presents bought for us for Christmas. The kind gestures shown to Mazy, who was going through just as much as we were. Our family was beyond blessed and shown so much grace during a time that was filled with many trials and triumphs.

After my post-operation visit mid-December, I finally had all restrictions lifted. That meant I could lift Mazy again and drive. Two things that, after two months of not doing, became glorious reintroductions into my life. The moment I picked up Mazy for the first time, she looked at me with her bright blue eyes and said, "Mommy, you can hold me again!" Our snuggles and cuddles on the couch sure were precious during those two months of recovery, but there is something about physically holding your child. She knew where every incision was, to be very careful about where she rested her head, and where she could hug me. Daily she would wake up asking if my owies were still there and unfortunately, the answer was always yes (and always will be since scars don't go away). But scars tell a story. A story that I can't wait to tell her about more fully someday.

After that appointment, Dan handed me the keys, while asking if I wanted to drive home. I wasn't sure I could drive the whole way home, but boy was I excited to get behind the wheel again!

I should say too, that Dan was exactly what I needed during this whole ordeal with my surgeries. Dan stayed by my side the entire hospital stay, for both surgeries. He relentlessly propped my pillows just so, so that I could start my night off comfortable. Day after day, he spoke with the doctors, trying to learn as much as he could about my situation, so that he could help me better understand what was happening. Day after day he encouraged me hour-by-hour to keep going, when the days seemed impossible. While at home, he would get up early, work, come home at lunch to help get Mazy down for a nap, go back to work, come home, and care for Mazy when I could not. He even slept in her room at night because she had such separation anxiety after we were gone for so many days. And he never *once* complained. His calm and patient demeanor carried our family during those difficult weeks and months of my recovery. His faithfulness and love to me during some of my darkest days in the hospital, puts me in awe of the gift that God has given me, in him.

Anyway, after all restrictions were lifted, I was also referred to a local hospital, Holland Hospital, to start outpatient cardiac rehabilitation. When the idea of rehab was brought up, I thought I was tough enough to do without it. Then after that second surgery, my struggle to walk normal during physical therapy sessions in the hospital, confirmed that I needed help. When the physical therapist asked me to walk normal and I couldn't, it was a wakeup call. My legs were unable to move as they should. I was unable to walk upright, but only hunched over, for lack of muscle in my neck, back, and core. Tipping my head back to any degree was impossible. I had lost an incredible amount of strength in my legs, arms, torso, chest, and neck. Retraining my body to work appropriately, could only happen through rehabilitation.

I walked into Holland Hospital for my first rehab appointment and found myself to be at an odd age. I was in a class with men about 30-40 years older than me, and one woman about 25 years older. As I watched them exercise, I realized I had so far to go. They were an inspiration to me as they sped up their treadmills and I stayed at the same speed. As my face probably showed my frustration, a kind gentleman said, "Hey, we were all beginners at one time too." I felt like it was a rough go at first, since one of my ribs was still broken. It frequently popped out of place, which hindered me from doing various stretches, weight lifting, and even some of the aerobic machines. Though the nurses and exercise physiologists gave me all the encouragement and education I needed to keep going. They helped give me the confidence I needed for life outside of rehab. And sure enough, within a few weeks, I was right there with the pack.

One of the most valuable lessons I learned while in rehab is that we all had the same goal: to make the most of our lives, despite our pasts. We were all there with different stories to tell. We all had different backgrounds. Different heart issues. Different lengths of stay in the hospital. But at 9:00 a.m., every Monday, Wednesday, and Friday, for ten weeks, we were all in it together. We were there to encourage each other and to laugh. Let's be honest, it maybe wasn't our first choice of places to be three times a week, but in the end, it became mine. There was no other group of people I was so excited to see on a weekly basis. Rehab gave me the mental and physical assurance I needed to keep moving forward.

The months following rehab were frustrating in the sense that my body still retained fluid, for unknown reasons. I was told it could take a year for my body to regulate itself and even to feel like myself again. It was difficult to comprehend that even after two open heart surgeries that my heart still wasn't doing what it was supposed to do, but in the end, it's not about what my heart can and can't do. It's all about what God is doing. I will indeed need another surgery someday to replace my cow's valve, but the timing of that is not in my hands. Just like everything else in life.

After my first surgery, I was told I would go on to live a "normal" life. Having two open heart surgeries in 17 days wasn't part of the original plan. What ended up being plan B in my mind was God's plan A all along.

We can all think back to a time in our lives when things didn't go according to plan for various reasons. Maybe the weather was to blame. Maybe someone didn't make a good choice and their consequences affected not only them, but you too. Maybe you have no answer as to why you are at plan B in your life.

What if there wasn't anything such as a plan B? What if "this" was the plan all along? Why did God allow a congenital heart defect to now affect most of my life? Why the losses? Why two surgeries so close together?

Isaiah 55:8-9 says, "For my thoughts are not your thoughts, neither are your ways my ways," declares the Lord. "As the heavens are higher than the earth, so are my ways higher than your ways and my thoughts than your thoughts."

It is not a plan B. It was God's plan all along and it should be ours too. I know our lives feel like shifting sand sometimes. Unsteady, unpredictable, wondering where it's going to land us. The thing of it is, God's ways are so much higher than ours. The very God who created every single leaf, on every single tree, put it there for a reason. The very God who decided to create galaxies far beyond the human eye can see, also created that little baby inside a mother. Both unseen, without an assistive device. This same God knew that a congenital heart defect would pave an incredibly uncertain, unbelievable, and unexplainable story in my life, not for my glory, but for His alone.

I could never have made this story up in my head. I'm sure you could say the same for your life too. Life takes you on many twists and turns, that have you gripping the steering wheel, leaving nothing but the sweat from your hands on the wheel. It is a wild ride, folks. When you feel that wild ride leaving tire marks on the road, take a glance back, but don't let that define your journey. Keep looking ahead. There is an open road, waiting for you to drive on.

Picture in your mind the most stunning scene you have laid your eyes on. For me, it is the tapestry of mountains on the horizon, with the sun peering through the cracks between them. If driving, I want to speed up to get to them faster, but in reality, they are hours and hours away. We want to soak in all the beauty of them and just can't wait to get there, right?

Isn't it odd to think that some of the most beautiful places on this earth are mountains? Yet figuratively speaking, mountains are what we dread most in life; the mountains known as obstacles, difficulties, and challenges. When we look up at them, when it comes to our circumstances, they seem insurmountable and impassable. What we forget to look for though, in EVERY mountain we face, is that crack towards the top, with the Son peeking in. God is not

225

standing behind this mountain, waiting for us to come around the corner though; He is actually right there in the midst, guiding us along, if we are just willing to look up.

CHAPTER 26

A Heartbeat of Grace

I struggled to come up with a title for this book. I couldn't think of one that fully enfolded every aspect of our story and summed it up into one nice and neat title. One day it dawned on me though: A Heartbeat of Grace. Indeed, those four words were a summary of my entire life.

I was born with a congenital heart defect that required heart surgery. I experienced the pain of being told I couldn't have my own children, only to get my hopes up and then dashed with the loss of two beautiful babies, before they were born. Soon after came the sorrow of leaving everything that is familiar and starting over. Then I experienced the physical, emotional, and spiritual agony of going through two open heart surgeries in a little over two weeks. While in the midst of it all, it was sometimes hard to see God's grace.

Then I look back at what God has done in my life. The utter grace He has showered on me. Brenda had sent me a text one day that so beautifully summed up what God's grace looks like, when reflecting on the loss we went through together:

"I believe God wanted us each to wrestle with different things; to grow us and to bring us perfectly to the place He wanted. His purposes were accomplished. God, in spite of us, accomplished His purpose. Was there pain? Yes. Was there struggle? Yes. Am I better person because of our journey together? Yes. We do not regret any of it. Maybe it was about what God wanted us to learn about Him. Maybe it was so that we could see His power at work in different ways. It is deep healing for all of us, to learn that He far exceeds the box we try to put him in, to realize He is completely trustworthy, and that He had plans for places for us to serve. It's a journey of growth, faith, and healing. As I look back at this time in my life, God moved in ways I was unable to see. Even when I was in the dark place of deep pain, He was orchestrating a plan more beautiful than I could ever imagine. He has overwhelmed me with His grace and goodness, not because there is anything special about me, but because that is the essence of who God is. He is good and He is faithful."

When we fully understand what God's grace is, we can start to see Him working throughout our entire lives. Grace doesn't mean a free pass to an easy life or that we are somehow spared from any difficulties. When the Apostle Paul wrote the following in 2 Corinthians 12:9, a verse I have referenced before, we get a more accurate picture about what grace really is. "But he said to me, 'My grace is sufficient for you, for my power is made perfect in weakness.' Therefore, I will boast all the more gladly of my weaknesses, so that the power of Christ may rest upon me."

Leading up to that verse, Paul was afflicted by a thorn in his flesh. Though he prayed on three different occasions for God to remove it, the thorn remained. Among Christian circles, we often hear that it is God's will that everyone should be healthy and happy, and that if healing doesn't occur in answer to prayer, it's because a person lacks faith. This thinking runs contrary to Paul's experience though. Without a doubt, Paul had great faith, but his prayer for the removal of the thorn wasn't answered in the way he was asking. It's not that he didn't receive an answer, but the answer he received was, "My grace is sufficient for you." You see, the greatest answer to prayer is not the thing we pray for, but God Himself! We are so undeserving of God, but when God gives us more of Himself, *that* is grace.

God's power doesn't replace our weakness. What it does though, is it coincides with our weakness and comes to its full strength. The same suffering that reveals our weaknesses, reveals God's strength, "...for my power is made perfect in weakness." When we're at our lowest in human strength and have only God's power to sustain us, then we become avenues through which His power can be displayed. What a humbling act of grace.

In every struggle in my life, when I was to the point of not being able to do it on my own or didn't think I could take any more, God said, "Watch this, my grace is sufficient for you." I don't know what my future will look like, especially with regards to my heart; but what I do know is that with every beat of my heart, God's grace is magnified.

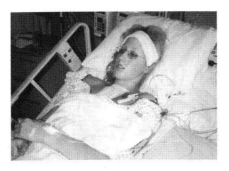

First open heart surgery in 2001

The beginning of our life together

Brenda carrying our twins

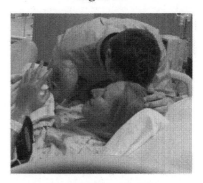

Our little miracle, Mazy Grace was born

Dr. Bolling and I; no wheelchair needed

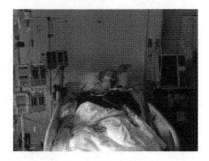

After my third open heart surgery

ACKNOWLEDGMENTS

Thanks to the encouragement of many, this book is now an extension of my heart and finally a story on paper. I want to thank these people for their hand in this book and walking this journey with me:

Dan, thank you for your wisdom, encouragement, and help in making this book come to life for me. Thank you for believing and dreaming with me.

Mazy, thank you for your patience, as I had to finish up "just one more paragraph." It is a true gift to be your mommy, every single day.

My parents, thank you for setting an example of selfless love and what a commitment to Christ looks like on a daily basis. Your legacy of faith has been incredibly influential in my life and always will be.

My sisters, Kari and Katie, thank you for your support, listening ears, and inspiration in this whole process. Your belief in me, gave me the confidence I needed to make this dream a reality.

Mary Alice, thank you for being my relentless editor, but even more so, for investing in me, praying for me, and for being my 'Bama Buddy! Thank you for teaching me to look for the still, small, and tangible ways in which God works in my life.

Matt and Brianna, thank you for the laughs, the faith talks, for walking with us on our journey, and encouraging us to write this story.

Tim and Brenda, thank you for your faith and obedience to God's will, which we believe, through God's providential hand, has led us to this beautiful place in our life. The days of us talking about writing a book and telling our story, have finally come true. Thank you for your commitment to Him and for your friendship that has never wavered.

Our families, thank you for walking with us on our journey and for cheering us on with this book.

My friends, you know who you are, thank you for helping me with all those little details when I just couldn't make a decision.

My faithful blog readers: thank you for encouraging me in my writing!

And finally, to everyone who has spoken the words "write a book" to us. Without that push and without your reassurance, this book wouldn't have come to fruition.

THANK YOU.

NOTES

1. "Congenital Heart Defects." *Centers for Disease Control and Prevention.* January 8, 2018.
    https://www.cdc.gov/ncbddd/heartdefects/data.html

2. Mancini, Mary C. "Anomalous Left Coronary Artery from the Pulmonary Artery." *Medscape.* January 17, 2017.
    https://emedicine.medscape.com/article/893290-overview.

3. Al Umairi, Rashid Saif. "Anomalous Origin of the Left Coronary Artery from the Pulmonary Artery: The Role of Multislice Computed Tomography (MSCT)." *Oman Medical Journal.* September 2016: 31(5): 387-389.
    https://www.ncbi.nlm.nih.gov/pmc/articles/PMC4996953/.

4. "Chapters and Verses of the Bible." *Wikipedia: The Free Encyclopedia.* January 25, 2018.
    https://en.wikipedia.org/wiki/Chapters_and_verses_of_the_Bible.

5. "What Is Heart Failure?" *American Heart Association.* March 7, 2018.
    http://www.heart.org/HEARTORG/Conditions/HeartFailure/AboutHeartFailure/What-is-Heart-Failure_UCM_002044_Article.jsp#.WmeFjq6nHIU.

6. Young, Sarah. *Jesus Calling.* Nashville: Thomas Nelson, 2004. Print.

7. The Heidelberg Catechism. *Psalter Hymnal.* Kalamazoo, Michigan: CRC Publications. 1987: 861.

8. Christian Reformed Church. *Acts of Synod*. Grand Rapids, MI: Christian Reformed Church of North America. Pg. 633.

9. Young, Sarah. *Jesus Calling*. Nashville: Thomas Nelson, 2004. Print.

10. Swindoll, Chuck. "The Impossible Is God's Ideal." *Insight For Today*. May 16, 2017. http://www.insight.org/resources/daily-devotional/individual/the-impossible-is-god-s-ideal.

11. Barber, Wayne; Eddie Rasnake; Richard Shepherd. *Life Principles From The Old Testament*. Chattanooga: AMG Publishers. 2012.

12. "Mitral Valve Disease." *Frankel Cardiovascular Center: University of Michigan*. 2017. https://www.umcvc.org/conditions-treatments/mitral-valve-repair-and-treatment.

13. "Improving Survival In Patients With Mitral Valve Regurgitation." *Colleagues in Care: University of Michigan*. February 11, 2016. http://umcic.org/2016/02/11/improving-survival-in-patients-with-mitral-valve-regurgitation.

Made in the USA
Columbia, SC
09 June 2018